VOGUE KNITTING

BABY KNITS
TWO

VOGUE KNITTING

BABY KNITS TWO

SIXTH&SPRING BOOKS
NEW YORK

SIXTH&SPRING BOOKS
233 Spring Street
New York, New York 10013

Copyright© 2004 by Sixth&Spring Books
All rights reserved including the right of reproduction
in whole or in part in any form.

Library of Congress Cataloging-in-Publication Data

Baby knits two.
      p. cm. -- (Vogue knitting on the go!)
      ISBN 1-931543-50-X
      1. Knitting--Patterns. 2. Infants' clothing I. Series.

TT825.B29323 2004
746.43'20432--dc22   2003067328

Manufactured in China

1 3 5 7 9 10 8 6 4 2

First Edition

TABLE OF CONTENTS

INTRODUCTION

Recently, people have come to call knitting "the new yoga," meaning that it is the latest trend to encourage relaxation, meditation, and enlightenment in a world of ever-increasing stress. While this may be a lot of pressure to put on one's in-progress sweater or scarf, there is some truth to this characterization; the rhythmic and creative experience of knitting is indeed soothing. However, finding the time to take part in this calming activity can be a challenge; if you're short on time, the idea of beginning a pullover or jacket is a daunting prospect, no matter how rewarding the results.

We understand this dilemma all too well; after all, we're busy knitters too. That's why we felt it was time for another edition of Baby Knits. When you're short on time, making garments for little ones gives you the benefits of knitting without the long-term, long-houred commitment, and better yet, without the cost. You can enjoy beautiful colors, lush textures, and high-quality patterns from some of our best designers in projects that fit your budget in every way. All you have to do is flip through this collection to see what you can accomplish on a smaller scale—the ethnic stateliness of the Asian-Inspired Baby Set; the floral delicacy of the Fair Isle Cardigan and Booties; or the adorably knitted Bears in Pajamas.

Whatever you choose for your next project, it is guaranteed that *Baby Knits Two* will give you the best of knitting in a fraction of the time. So pick out some yarn, pick up some needles and get ready to **KNIT ON THE GO!**

THE BASICS

Baby knits are perfect for both beginning and experienced knitters. Novices appreciate the manageable size and the speed with which they can create their first projects, while seasoned stitchers love the personal touch they can add to the typical baby gift. And just like adult styles, baby knits come in a wide array of yarns, textures, colors and designs, making choosing your project just as exciting as any other. No matter what you knit or whom it's for, we're sure you'll be enchanted by the endearing designs that fill these pages.

SIZING

Most of the garments in this book are written for sizes 6 months through 24 months, with extra ease for your child to grow into the sweater. You will notice a big jump in sleeve length from size 18 months to 24 months. This is because the 24-month size is a transition from baby sizes to toddler sizes. Since children's measurements change so rapidly, it is best to measure your child or a sweater that fits them well to determine which size to make.

YARN SELECTION

For an exact reproduction of the projects photographed, use the yarn listed in the materials section of the pattern. We've chosen yarns that are readily available in the U.S. and Canada at the time of printing. The Resources list on pages 94 and 95 provides addresses of yarn distributors. Contact them for the name of a retailer in your area.

YARN SUBSTITUTION

You may wish to substitute yarns. You'll need to knit to the given gauge to obtain the knitted measurements with a substitute yarn (see "Gauge" on page 11). Be sure to consider how the fiber content of the substitute yarn will affect the comfort and the ease of care of your projects.

To facilitate yarn substitution, Vogue Knitting grades yarn by the standard stitch gauge obtained in Stockinette stitch. You'll find a grading number in the "Materials" section of the pattern, immediately following the the yarn information. Look for a substitute yarn that falls into the same category. The suggested needle size and gauge on the ball band should be comparable to that on the Standard Yarn Weight chart on page 12.

After you've successfully gauge-swatched a substitute yarn, you'll need to figure out how much of the substitute yarn the project requires. First, find the total length of the original yarn in the pattern (multiply number of balls by yards/meters per ball). Divide this figure by the new yards/meters per ball (listed on the ball band). Round up to the next whole number. The answer is the number of balls required.

FOLLOWING CHARTS

Charts are a convenient way to follow colorwork, lace, cable and other stitch patterns at a glance. Vogue Knitting stitch charts utilize the universal knitting language of "symbolcraft." When knitting in the round, read charts from right to left

It is always important to knit a gauge swatch, and it is even more so with garments or they will not fit properly. If your gauge is too loose, you could end up with an over-sized garment, if it's too tight, the garment will be too small.

Patterns usually state gauge over a 4"/10cm span, however it's beneficial to make a larger test swatch. This gives a more precise stitch gauge, a better idea of the appearance and drape of the knitted fabric, and gives you a chance to familiarize yourself with the stitch pattern.

Measure the gauge over 4"/10cm. Try different needle sizes until your sample measures the required number of stitches and rows. *To get fewer stitches to the inch/cm, use larger needles; to get more stitches to the inch/cm, use smaller needles.*

on every round, repeating any stitch and row repeats as directed in the pattern. When knitting back and forth in rows, read charts from right to left on right side (RS) rows and from left to right on wrong side (WS) rows. Posting a self-adhesive note under your working row is an easy way to keep track of your place on a chart.

Two main types of colorwork are explored in this book.

Intarsia
Intarsia is accomplished with separate bobbins of individual colors. This method is ideal for large blocks of color or for motifs that aren't repeated close together, such as the Giraffe Cardigan on page 20. When changing colors, always pick up the new color and wrap it around the old color to prevent holes.

Stranding
When motifs are closely placed, colorwork is accomplished by stranding along two or more colors per row, creating "floats" on the wrong side of the fabric. This technique is sometimes called Fair Isle knitting, after the traditional Fair Isle patterns composed of small motifs with frequent color changes.

Blocking is an all-important finishing step in the knitting process. Most garments retain their shape after pressing if the blocking stages in the instructions are followed carefully.

Using rust-proof pins, pin pieces to measurements on a flat surface and lightly dampen using a spray bottle. Allow to dry before removing pins.

With WS facing, pin pieces to measurements. Steam lightly, holding the iron 2"/5cm above the knitting. Do not press, as it will flatten stitches.

Categories of yarn, gauge ranges and recommended needle and hook sizes

Yarn Weight Symbol & Category Names	**① Super Fine**	**② Fine**	**③ Light**	**④ Medium**	**⑤ Bulky**	**⑥ Super Bulky**
Type of Yarns in Category	Sock, Fingering, Baby	Sport, Baby	DK, Light Worsted	Worsted, Afghan, Aran	Chunky, Craft, Rug	Super Bulky, Roving
Knit Gauge Range* in Stockinette Stitch to 4 inches	27–32 sts	23–26 sts	21–24 sts	16–20 sts	12–15 sts	6–11 sts
Recommended Needle in Metric Size Range	2.25–3.25 mm	3.25–3.75 mm	3.75–4.5 mm	4.5–5.5 mm	5.5–8 mm	9–15 mm and larger
Recommended Needle U.S. size range	1 to 3	3 to 5	5 to 7	7 to 9	9 to 11	11 to 19 and larger
Crochet Gauge* Ranges in Single Crochet to 4 inch	21–32 sts	16–20 sts	12–17 sts	11–14 sts	8–11 sts	5–9 sts
Recommended Hook in Metric Size Range	2.25–3.5 mm	3.5–4.5 mm	4.5–5.5 mm	5.5–6.5 mm	6.5–9 mm	9–12 mm and larger
Recommended Hook U.S. Size Range	B-1 to E-4	E-4 to 7	7 to I-9	I-9 to K-10½	K-10½ to M-13	M-13 to P-16 and larger

SKILL LEVELS FOR KNITTING

Beginner

Ideal first project.

Intermediate

For knitters with some experience. More intricate stitches, shaping and finishing.

■■☐☐☐

Very Easy Very Vogue

Basic stitches, minimal shaping, simple finishing.

■■■■

Experienced

For knitters able to work patterns with complicated shaping and finishing.

KNITTING TERMS AND ABBREVIATIONS

approx approximately

beg begin(ning)

bind off Used to finish an edge and keep stitches from unraveling. Lift the first stitch over the second, the second over the third, etc. (UK: cast off)

cast on A foundation row of stitches placed on the needle in order to begin knitting.

CC contrast color

ch chain(s)

cm centimeter(s)

cn cable needle

cont continu(e)(ing)

dc double crochet (UK: tr-treble)

dec decrease(ing)—Reduce the stitches in a row (knit 2 together).

dpn double pointed needle(s)

foll follow(s)(ing)

g gram(s)

garter stitch Knit every row. Circular knitting: knit one round, then purl one round.

hdc half-double crochet (UK: htr-half treble)

inc increase(ing)—Add stitches in a row (knit into the front and back of a stitch).

k knit

k2tog knit 2 stitches together

lp(s) loops(s)

LH left-hand

m meter(s)

M1 make one stitch—With the needle tip, lift the strand between last stitch worked and next stitch on the left-hand needle and knit into the back of it. One stitch has been added.

MC main color

mm millimeter(s)

oz ounce(s)

p purl

p2tog purl 2 stitches together

pat pattern

pick up and knit (purl) Knit (or purl) into the loops along an edge.

pm place marker—Place or attach a loop of contrast yarn or purchased stitch marker as indicated.

rem remain(s)(ing)

rep repeat

rev St st reverse Stockinette stitch—Purl right-side rows, knit wrong-side rows. Circular knitting: purl all rounds. (UK: reverse stocking stitch)

rnd(s) round(s)

RH right-hand

RS right side(s)

sc single crochet (UK: dc - double crochet)

sk skip

SKP Slip 1, knit 1, pass slip stitch over knit 1.

SK2P Slip 1, knit 2 together, pass slip stitch over k2tog.

sl slip—An unworked stitch made by passing a stitch from the left-hand to the right-hand needle as if to purl.

sl st slip stitch (UK: single crochet)

ssk slip, slip, knit—Slip next 2 stitches knitwise, one at a time, to right-hand needle. Insert tip of left-hand needle into fronts of these stitches from left to right. Knit them together. One stitch has been decreased.

st(s) stitch(es)

St st Stockinette stitch—Knit right-side rows, purl wrong-side rows. Circular knitting: knit all rounds. (UK: stocking stitch)

tbl through back of loop

tog together

tr treble crochet (UK: dtr-double treble)

WS wrong side(s)

w&t wrap and turn

wyif with yarn in front

wyib with yarn in back

work even Continue in pattern without increasing or decreasing. (UK: work straight)

yd yard(s)

yo yarn over—Make a new stitch by wrapping the yarn over the right-hand needle. (UK: yfwd, yon, yrn)

* Repeat directions following * as many times as indicated.

[ ] Repeat directions inside brackets as many times as indicated.

This plaid patterned romper with sailor collar abounds with details in structure and finish. Designed by Svetlana Avrahk.

SIZES
Instructions are written for size 3 months. Changes for sizes 6 months and 12 months are in parentheses.

KNITTED MEASUREMENTS
* Chest 22½ (25, 27)"/57 (64, 68)cm
* Length 18¾ (20¼, 23½)"/47.5 (51.5, 59.5)cm
* Upper arm 9¼ (10, 11¼)"/23 (26, 29)cm

MATERIALS
* 2 (3, 3) 1¾oz/50g Patons® *Bumblebee* 123yd/112m (cotton) in # 02005 white (MC)
* 2 balls in # 02129 lt blue (CC) (4)
* One pair each sizes 5 and 7 (3.75 and 4.5mm) needles *or size to obtain gauge*
* Nine ⅜-inch/10mm buttons
* Stitch holders

GAUGE
20 sts and 26 rows to 4"/10cm over St st using larger needles.
Take time to check gauge.

BACK
Left leg
With smaller needles and A, cast on 21 (23, 27) sts.

Row 1 (RS) K1, *p1, k1; rep from * to end.

Row 2 P1, *k1, p1; rep from * to end.

Rep these 2 rows for k1, p1 rib for a total of 6 rows, inc 1 st at center of last WS row—22 (24, 28) sts. Change to larger needles.

Beg chart pat
Note Red outlines indicate size 3 months, yellow outlines indicate size 6 months and black outlines indicate size 12 months. Work foll chart for chosen size through row 46—30 (34, 38) sts. Cut yarn. Leave sts on a spare needle.

Right leg
Work as for left leg with ribbing then foll chart—30 (34, 38) sts on row 46. Do not cut yarn.

Join legs
Next row (RS) Work row 47 of chart casting on 4 sts at center to join—64 (72, 80) sts. Cont to foll chart with side shaping as on chart, through row 128 (134, 144). There are 56 (62, 68) sts.

Neck shaping
Next row (RS) Work 21 (22, 25) sts, place center 14 (18, 18) sts on a holder, join a 2nd ball of yarn and work to end. Working both sides at once, dec 1 st each side *every* row 3 times—18 (19, 22) sts each side. When chart is completed, bind off sts each side for shoulders.

FRONT
Work as for back foll chart through row 110 (112, 118).

V-neck shaping

Next row (RS) Work 27 (30, 33) sts, join a 2nd ball of yarn and bind off center 2 sts, work to end. Working both sides at once, dec 1 st each side of neck *every* row 6 (4, 2) times, every 2nd row 3 (7, 9) times—18 (19, 22) sts rem each side. Complete chart as for back.

SLEEVES
With smaller needles and A, cast on 33 (35, 37) sts. Work in k1, p1 rib for 6 rows, inc 5 sts evenly spaced on last WS row—38 (40, 42) sts. Change to larger needles and cont in St st, inc 1 st each side every 4th row 4 (5, 7) times—46 (50, 56) sts. Work even until piece measures 5½ (6½, 7½)"/14 (16.5, 19) cm from beg. Bind off

SAILOR COLLAR
Sew shoulder seams.

Left collar extension

With larger needles and A, cast on 2 sts. K 1 row, p 1 row.

Next row (RS) Inc 1 st in first st, k1—3 sts. P 1 row.

Next row Inc 1 st in first st, k to end of row – 4 sts. P 1 row.

Rep last 2 rows 4 (2, 4) times more – 8 (6, 8) sts

Next row Inc 1 st in first st, k to end of row—9 (7, 9) sts. P 1 row, k 1 row, p 1 row.

Rep last 4 rows 1 (3, 2) times more—10 (10, 11) sts. Cut yarn. Sl sts to a holder.

Right collar extension

With larger needles and A, cast on 2 sts. K 1 row, p 1 row.

Next row (RS) Inc 1 st in first st, k1—3 sts. P 1 row.

Next row K1, inc 1 st in next st, k1—4 sts. P 1 row.

Next row K to last 2 sts, inc 1 st in next st, k1—5 sts. P 1 row.

Rep last 2 rows 3 (1, 3) times more—8 (6, 8) sts.

Next row K to last 2 sts, inc 1 st in next st, k1. P 1 row, k 1 row, p 1 row.

Rep last 4 rows 1 (3, 2) times more—10 (10, 11) sts.

Joining row

With WS of romper neck matching RS of collar and with A, k 10 (10, 11) from left collar extension, pick up and p 5 sts down left back neck edge, p 14 (18, 18) from back neck holder, pick up and p5 sts from right back neck edge, k 10 (10, 11) from right collar extension—44 (48, 50) sts. Pm to mark end of row. Beg with a purl row, work in St st until collar measures 4 (4½, 5)"/10 (11.5, 12.5) cm, end with a WS row. With smaller needles and B, *k 1 row, inc 1 st each end of row. K 1 row with B; rep from * once, then k next row with B, inc 1 st each side of row—50 (54, 56) sts. Bind off knitwise.

Right collar trim and tie

With RS facing, smaller needles and B, pick up and k 40 (46, 51) sts along right side of collar.

Row 1 (WS) Cast on 15 sts (for tie), k to last 2 sts, inc 1 st in next st, k1.

Row 2 Inc 1 st in first st, k to end.

Row 3 K to last 2 sts, inc 1 st in next st, k1.

Row 4 Rep row 2. Bind off.

Left collar trim and tie

With smaller needles and B, cast on 15 sts, then with RS of collar facing, pick up and k 40 (46, 51) sts along left side of collar. Complete as for right collar trim in reverse.

Ring

With smaller needles and A, cast on 15 sts. K 4 rows. Bind off. Sew ends tog to form ring.

V-Inset

With larger needles and A, cast on 5 sts.

Row 1 (RS) Inc 1 st in first st, k to last 2 sts, inc 1 st in next st, k1. P 1 row.

Rep last 2 rows 9 times more—25 sts. Change to smaller needles and B.

Buttonhole row (RS) K1, k2tog, yo, k to last 3 sts, yo, k2tog, k1. K 2 rows. Bind off.

Buttonhole leg trim

With front of romper facing, using smaller needles and A pick up and k 31 (34, 42) sts up front right leg opening, 4 sts at crotch, 31 (34, 43) sts along front left leg opening—66 (72, 89) sts. K1 row.

Buttonhole row (RS) K3 (3, 2), [yo, k2tog, k 8 (9, 12)] 6 times, yo k2tog, k1. K 2 rows. Bind off knitwise. Work button band trim on the back legs, omitting buttonholes, in the same way.

FINISHING

Block to measurements. Sew collar fronts to V-neck edge. Insert front ties into ring. Sew on 2 buttons under the collar to match the V-inset and button inset through buttons. Place markers at 4½ (5, 5½)"/ 11.5 (13, 14.5)cm down from shoulders. Sew sleeves to armholes between markers. Sew side and sleeve seams. Sew on buttons.

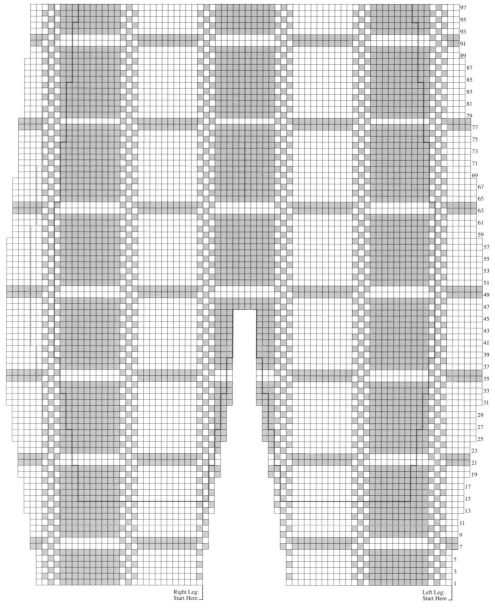

Right Leg:
Start Here

Left Leg:
Start Here

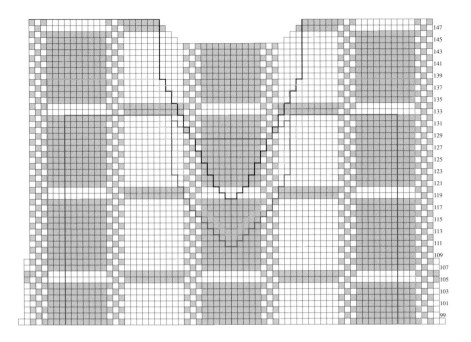

Color Key

☐ (MC)

▨ (CC)

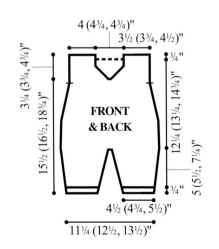

4 (4¾, 4¾)"

3½ (3¾, 4½)"

¾"

3¼ (3¾, 4¾)"

15½ (16½, 18¾)"

12¼ (13¼, 14¾)"

FRONT & BACK

5 (5½, 7¼)"

¾"

4½ (4¾, 5½)"

11¼ (12½, 13½)"

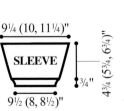

9¼ (10, 11¼)"

SLEEVE

4¾ (5¾, 6¾)"

¾"

9½ (8, 8½)"

GIRAFFE CARDIGAN AND HAT
Hit the road

Easy cardigan styling gets a boost with bright color graphics, fun buttons and dimensional appliqués. Design is by Amy Bahrt.

GAUGE

18 sts and 24 rows to 4"/10cm over St st using larger needles.
Take time to check gauge.

STRIPE PAT FOR HAT

Working in St st, work 4 rows C, 4 rows B, 4 rows A, 4 rows B, 4 rows D, 4 rows B, 4 rows E (28 rows), work in B to end.

SIZES

Instructions for cardigan are written for size 12 months. Changes for sizes 18 and 24 months are in parentheses. Hat is one size.

KNITTED MEASUREMENTS

CARDIGAN
- Chest (buttoned) 24½ (27, 29¼)"/62 (68.5, 74.5)cm
- Length 11 (12½, 14)"/28 (32, 35.5)cm
- Upper arm 10¼ (11¼, 12)"/26 (28, 31)cm

HAT
- Head circumference 16"/40cm

MATERIALS
- 2 (3, 3) 1¾oz/50g balls (each approx 74yd/67m) of Tahki Yarns/Tahki•Stacy Charles, Inc. *Cotton Classic II* (cotton) in #2871 royal blue (A)
- 4 balls in #2847 med blue (B)
- 1 ball each in #2726 green (C), #2997 red (D), #2533 yellow (E), #2486 orange (F) and #2002 black (G)
- One pair each sizes 5 and 7 (3.75 and 4.5mm) needles *or size to obtain gauge*
- Size D (3.25mm) crochet hook
- Small piece of yellow felt
- Stitch holder
- Four ½-inch/13mm decorative buttons and two white four-hole buttons for car wheels

CARDIGAN

BACK

With smaller needles and B, cast on 54 (58, 64) sts. Work in k1, p1 rib for 1¼"/3cm. Change to larger needles and C. Work in St st for 2 rows.
Next row (RS) * K1 C, k2 A; rep from *, end K 0 (1, 1) C. With C, p 1 row, k 1 row. Change to A and work until piece measures 7 (8, 9)"/18 (20.5, 23) cm from beg.
Next row (RS) Work 0 (2, 2) sts B, *6 sts A, 2 sts B; rep from *, end 6 (0, 6) sts A. Work 1 row even in colors as established. Cont with B until piece measures 11 (12½, 14)"/28 (32, 35.5)cm from beg. Bind off 16 (18, 19) sts, work center 22 (22, 26) sts and place on holder, bind off rem sts.

LEFT FRONT

With smaller needles and B, cast on 26 (29, 32) sts. Work in k1, p1 rib for 1¼"/3cm. Change to larger needles and C. Work in St st for 2 rows.
Next row (RS) *K2 A, k1 C; rep from *, end k2 A. P 1 row, k 1 row with C.
Beg chart
Next row (WS) Work 2 (3, 4) sts A, beg with row 1, work chart over next 19 sts,

work in A to end. Cont as established, working chart for 25 rows. Change to A and work until piece measures 7 (8, 9)"/18 (20.5, 23)cm from beg, end with a WS row. **Next row (RS)** Work 8 (9, 11) sts A, 2 sts B, 6 sts A, 2 sts B, 8 (10, 11) sts A. Work 1 row even in colors as established. Cont in B until piece measures 8½ (10, 11½)"/21.5 (25.5, 29) cm from beg, end with a RS row.

Neck shaping

Next row (WS) Bind off 4 (5, 5) sts (neck edge), work to end. Cont to bind off from neck edge 2 sts 2 (2, 3) times, 1 st twice—16 (18, 19) sts. Work even until piece measures same as back to shoulder. Bind off rem sts for shoulder.

RIGHT FRONT

Work to correspond to left front, omitting chart (working chart section in A) and reversing all shaping.

SLEEVES

With smaller needles and B, cast on 30 sts. Work in k1, p1 rib for 1¼"/3cm. Change to larger needles, St st and C.

Next row (RS) K, inc 4 sts evenly spaced across—34 sts. Work 1 row even in C.

Next row (RS) *Work 1 st C, 2 sts A; rep from *, end 1 st C. Work 2 rows C. Change to larger needles and B. Cont in St st, inc 1 st each side every 4th row 6 (8, 10) times—46 (50, 54) sts. Work even until piece measures 6½ (8½, 10½)"/16.5 (21.5, 26.5)cm from beg. Bind off.

FINISHING

Block pieces to measurements. For eye, with A, form French knot (see page 87) as indicated on chart. For ears, with E, form french knots as indicated on chart. For scarf, with crochet hook and C, make a 4"/10cm chain and fasten to neck. Tie ends as in photo. Foll template, cut felt and sew in place as in photo. Sew shoulder seams.

Neckband

With smaller needles, RS facing and B, pick up and k58 (58, 62) sts evenly around neck edge, including back neck sts on holder. Work in k1, p1 rib for 1¼"/3cm. Bind off in rib.

Buttonband

Note

Work on left side for girls, on right side for boys. With smaller needles, RS facing and B, pick up and k52 (60, 66) sts evenly along front edge. Complete as for neckband. Place markers on band for 4 buttons, the first and last ones 1"/2.5cm from edges and the others spaced evenly between.

Buttonhole band

Work as for buttonband on opposite front edge for ½"/1.5cm, end with a WS row. Work buttonholes on next row opposite markers by binding off 2 sts for each buttonhole. On next row, cast on 2 sts over bound-off sts. Complete as for buttonband. Place markers 5 (5½, 6)"/13 (14, 15.5)cm down from shoulders on front and back. Sew sleeves between markers. Sew side and sleeve seams. Sew decorative buttons on front bands and four-hole buttons on wheels.

HAT

With smaller needles and B, cast on 77 sts. Work in k1, p1 rib for 1¼"/3cm. Change to larger needles. Work in stripe pat, AT SAME TIME, on row 17 beg dec for crown as foll:

Row 17 (RS) *K9, k2tog; rep from * to end—70 sts. Work 1 row even.

Row 19 *K8, k2tog; rep from * to end—63 sts. Work 1 row even.

Row 21 *K7, k2tog; rep from * to end—56 sts. Work 1 row even.

Row 23 *K6, k2tog; rep from * to end—49 sts. Work 1 row even.

Row 25 *K5, k2tog; rep from * to end—42 sts. Work 1 row even.

Row 27 *K4, k2tog; rep from * to end—35 sts. Work 1 row even.

Row 29 *K3, k2tog; rep from * to end – 28 sts. Work 1 row even.

Row 31 K2tog across—14 sts. Work 1 row even. Cut yarn, leaving end for sewing. Thread through rem sts and pull tightly to close. Sew back seam.

5 (5, 5¾)" 3½ (4, 4¼)"

11 (12½, 14)"

BACK

9¾ (11¼, 12¾)"

1¼"

12 (13, 14¼)"

3½ (4, 4¼)"

8½ (10, 11½)"

LEFT FRONT

11 (12½, 14)"

5¾ (6½, 7)"

10¼ (11¼, 12)"

SLEEVE

6½ (8½, 10½)"

6½"

felt appliqué template

Color Key

■ Royal Blue (A)
■ Red (D)
□ Yellow (E)
▨ Orange (F)
■ Black (G)

french knots in E   french knots in A

25
23
21
19
17
15
13
11
9
7
5
3
1

19 sts

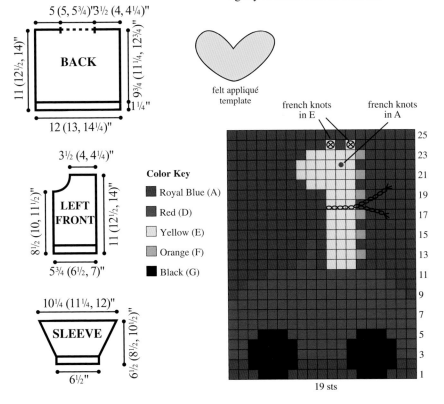

23

In just about an hour or so, make two, four or six of these adorable baby "driving" moccasins. Accented with knotted leather lacings, they're designed by Jean Guirguis.

SIZES

To fit sizes 6-12 months. For a smaller size (3-6 months) use one size smaller needles.

KNITTED MEASUREMENTS

■ Sole is 4½"/11.5cm long and shoe is 1½"/4cm deep at instep

MATERIALS

■ 1 4oz/113g skein (each approx 125yd/114m) of Brown Sheep Yarn Co. *Lamb's Pride Bulky* (wool/mohair) in #M-105 pink (A), #M-57 blue (B) or #M-110 orange (C) (5)

■ One set (5) size 10 (6mm) dpn *or size to obtain gauge*

■ 1yd/1m of leather laces in desired color

GAUGE

12 sts and 18 rows to 4"/10cm over St st using size 10 (6mm) dpn.
Take time to check gauge.

SOLE

With 2 dpn, beg at heel end, with desired color, cast on 5 sts.
Row 1 (RS) Knit.
Row 2 Purl.

Row 3 K1, M1, k1, M1, k1, M1, k2—8 sts. Work 3 rows even.
Row 7 K1, k2tog, k2, k2tog, k1—6 sts. Work 3 rows even.
Row 11 K2, M1, k2, M1, k2—8 sts. Work 1 row even.
Row 13 K3, M1, k2, M1, k3—10 sts. Work 5 rows even.
Row 19 K2, k2tog, k2, k2tog, k2—8 sts. Work 1 row even.
Row 21 K1, k2tog, k2, k2tog, k1 6—sts. Work 1 row even.
Row 23 [K2tog] twice, pull first st over 2nd st, k2tog and bind off.

SIDES

Using 3 dpn, beg at heel end, pick up and k 36 sts from RS all around the sole, having 12 sts on each of 3 needles. Join and pm for beg of rnd. K 3 rnds. Bind off.
Instep
(Instep will be worked back and forth in rows)
Return to the end of the shoe and pick up and k 3 sts.
Row 2 (WS) Purl.
Row 3 (RS) K1, M1, k1, M1, k1—5 sts.
Row 4 Purl.
Row 5 K1, M1, k1, M1, k1, M1, k2—8 sts. Work 5 rows even. Bind off knitwise.

FINISHING

Sew instep into the sides of the shoe front. Using crochet hook and leather lacing, work whip st over the instep joining and then knot as desired (see photo for 3 different ways to knot the leather lacing).

Garter strips in sunset hues and exposed seams are the elements that elevate this baby jacket to modern artwear. Easy-to-knit, the pieces all come together in this unique design construction by Linda Cyr.

Instructions are written for size 6 months. Changes for size 12 and 18 months are in parentheses.

KNITTED MEASUREMENTS

- Chest (buttoned) 20 (22, 24)"/51 (56, 61) cm
- Length (at side seam) 10½ (11¾, 13)"/26.5 (30, 33) cm
- Upper arm 8 (9, 10)"/21 (23, 25) cm

MATERIALS

- 2 1¾oz/50g skeins (each approx 138yd/123m) of Classic Elite Yarn *Waterspun* (wool) each in #2548 sunset (B) and #5051 gold (C) (4)
- 1 (1, 2) skeins in #5058 madden (A)
- Cable needle
- One pair size 6 (4mm) needles *or size to obtain gauge*
- Three ½-inch/13mm buttons

GAUGE

20 sts and 40 rows to 4"/10cm over garter st using size 6 (4mm) needles.
Take time to check gauge.

BACK YOKE

With A, cast on 52 (57, 62) sts.
Row 1 Sl 1 purlwise, yarn to back and k to end.
Rep this row until piece measures 6½ (7¼, 8)"/16.5 (18.5, 20.5)cm from beg. Bind off.

FRONT YOKE

(make 2)
With A, cast on 26 (29, 31) sts. Work garter st row 1 as for back until piece measures 4 (4½, 5)"/10 (11.5, 12.5)cm from beg. Bind off.

LEFT SIDE PANEL

With B, cast on 82 (90, 97) sts. Work garter st row 1 as for back until piece measures 6½ (7¼, 8)"/16.5 (18.5, 20.5)cm from beg. Bind off.

RIGHT SIDE PANEL

With C, cast on 82 (90, 97) sts. Work garter st row 1 as for back until piece measures 3¼ (3½, 4)"/8 (9, 10)cm from beg.
Buttonhole row 1 (RS) Sl 1 purlwise, yarn to back, k2, yo, ssk, k to end. Work even for 3 rows.
Buttonhole row 2 (RS) Sl 1, k7 (8, 9), yo, ssk, k to end. Work even until piece measures 6¼ (7, 7¾)"/15.5 (17.5, 19.5)cm from beg.
Buttonhole row 3 (RS) Sl 1, k2, yo, ssk, k to end. Work even for 3 rows (or until piece measures same as left side panel). Bind off.

SLEEVES

(make 1 in B and 1 in C)

Beg at top edge with B (C), cast on 42 (47, 52) sts.

Row 1 Sl 1 purlwise, yarn to back and k to end.

Rep this row 9 times more.

Row 7 Sl 1 purlwise, yarn to back, ssk, k to last 3 sts, ssk, k1.

Work even for 9 rows.

Rep last 10 rows 4 (5, 6) times more—32 (35, 38) sts. Piece measures approx 6 (7, 8)"/15 (18, 20.5)cm from beg. Bind off.

FINISHING

Block all pieces using steam block method. Mark 4 (4½, 5)"/10 (11.5, 12.5)cm at top of center back yoke for neck opening. Sewing seams with selvage on RS, sew front yoke shoulder seams to back yoke so that 2 (2¼, 2½)"/5 (5.5, 6.5)cm will be left free at center front neck for lapels. Place yarn markers at 2½"/16.5cm down from top of lapels on center fronts. Pin or baste right side panel (in C) with left corner to lower left corner of back yoke, then overlapping front panel over back yoke, pin to front panel even at front yoke side seam, then match end of side panel to yarn marker (at lapel center). The right side panel (in C) now overlaps the front and back yokes (in A) and the fold line for side seam will form a straight edge and the lower edges will angle as in photo. The left side panel (in B) will be placed on top of the right panel with the first point at the right side seam (see photo), angling the piece upwards and the left side seam point at underarm point, the final center front joining point at yarn marker at lapel. Sew in place. Fold sleeves in half lengthwise and sew to armholes in the 4 (4½, 5)"/10.5 (11.5, 12.5)cm opening each side. Sew side seams with selvages showing. With left side panel in place, sew on buttons to match buttonholes. Fold back lapels and press flat (as in photo).

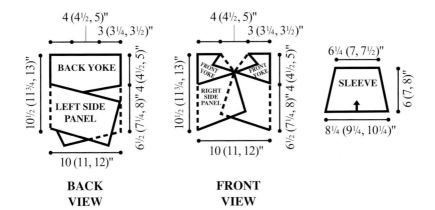

4 (4½, 5)"

3 (3¼, 3½)"

10½ (11¾, 13)"

BACK YOKE

LEFT SIDE PANEL

6½ (7¼, 8)" 4 (4½, 5)"

10 (11, 12)"

**BACK
VIEW**

4 (4½, 5)"

3 (3¼, 3½)"

10½ (11¾, 13)"

FRONT YOKE

FRONT YOKE

RIGHT SIDE PANEL

6½ (7¼, 8)" 4 (4½, 5)"

10 (11, 12)"

**FRONT
VIEW**

6¼ (7, 7½)"

SLEEVE

6 (7, 8)"

8¼ (9¼, 10¼)"

Baby's first faux

Just a few stitches and rows are all it takes to work up this quick-to-knit baby's coat. The yarn does all the work, creating a deep fake fur-like fabric. Designed by Jean Guirguis.

SIZES
Instructions are written for size 6 months. Changes for sizes 12, 18 and 24 months are in parentheses.

KNITTED MEASUREMENTS
▓ Chest (buttoned) 22 (23½, 25, 27)"/56 (59.5, 63.5, 68.5)cm
▓ Length 10 (11, 12½, 14)"/25.5 (28, 32, 35.5)cm
▓ Upper arm 9½ (10½, 11½, 12½)"/24 (27, 29, 32)cm

MATERIALS
▓ 5 1¾oz/50g balls (each approx 27yd/ 25m) of Gedifra/KFI *Mambo Acrylic Polyamid* in #796 burnt orange (**6**)
▓ One pair size 11 (8mm) needles *or size to obtain gauge*
▓ One set (4) size 11 (8mm) dpn
▓ Three 1"/25mm buttons
▓ Stitch holders, stitch markers

GAUGE
10 sts and 16 rows to 4"/10cm over garter st using size 11 (8mm) needles.
Take time to check gauge.

BACK
With A, cast on 26 (28, 30, 32) sts. Work in garter st for 10 (11, 12½, 14)"/25.5 (28, 32, 35.5)cm. Place 7 (8, 9, 9) sts on first holder for shoulder, 12 (12, 12, 14) sts on 2nd holder for neck and 7 (8, 9, 9) sts on a 3rd holder for 2nd shoulder.

LEFT FRONT
Cast on 15 (16, 17, 18) sts. Work in garter st for 8½ (9½, 10½, 12)"/21.5 (24, 26.5, 30.5)cm, end with a RS row.

Neck shaping
Next row (WS) Bind off 2 (2, 2, 3) sts, work to end. Cont to shape neck binding off 2 sts from neck edge 3 times more. Work even, if necessary, until piece measures same length as back. Sl 7 (8, 9, 9) sts to a holder for shoulder.
Place markers for 3 buttons, the first one at ½"/1.5cm from neck edge and the other 2 at 1½"/4cm intervals.

RIGHT FRONT
Work as for left front (pattern is reversible) only working 3 buttonholes opposite markers at 3 sts from center edge by k2, yo, k2tog for each buttonhole.
Join shoulder seams
Sl shoulder sts onto 2 dpn and from WS, k1 st of front shoulder tog with 1 st of back shoulder and then bind off each st for a 3-needle bind-off (see page 77).
SLEEVES
Place markers for sleeves at 4¾ (5¼, 5¾,

6¼)"/12 (13.5, 14.5, 16)cm down from shoulders. Pick up and k 24 (26, 28, 31) sts between markers. Work in garter st on these sts for 4 rows. Dec 1 st each side of next row. Rep dec every other row 3 (4, 4, 5) times more—16 (16, 18, 19) sts. Work even until sleeve measures 5 (5½, 7, 8½)"/12.5 (14, 18, 21.5)cm. Bind off.

Collar

From RS, pick up and k 9 (9, 9, 10) sts from right front neck, 12 (12, 12, 14) sts from back neck holder, 9 (9, 9, 10) sts from left front neck—30 (30, 30, 34) sts. Work in garter st for 4"/10cm. Bind off. Sew side and sleeve seams. Sew on buttons.

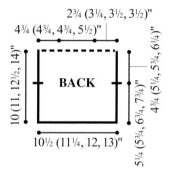

2¾ (3¼, 3½, 3½)"

4¾ (4¾, 4¾, 5½)"

10 (11, 12½, 14)"

BACK

4¾ (5¼, 5¾, 6¼)"

5¼ (5¾, 6¾, 7¾)"

10½ (11¼, 12, 13)"

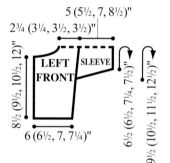

5 (5½, 7, 8½)"

2¾ (3¼, 3½, 3½)"

8½ (9½, 10½, 12)"

LEFT FRONT **SLEEVE**

6½ (6½, 7¼, 7½)"

9½ (10½, 11½, 12½)"

6 (6½, 7, 7¼)"

32

FELTED BABY BAG
Full of it

The felting process is the finishing technique that brings about the soft fabric used to make up this tote bag. Featuring shoulder and tote handles, this Jil Eaton design is worked in two shades of blue.

KNITTED MEASUREMENTS

▥ Pre-felted: 16"/40cm high x 20½"/52cm long x 8½"/21.5cm deep

▥ After felting: 8½"/21.5cm high x 17"/43cm long x 6½"/16.5cm deep

MATERIALS

▥ 2 3½oz/100g skeins (each approx 138yd/127m) of Manos del Uruguay *Manos* (wool) in #60 french blue (A) (⬛)

▥ 4 skeins in #05 aqua (B)

▥ One pair size 10½ (6.5mm) needles *or size to obtain gauge*

▥ Size 10½ (6.5mm) dpn

▥ Tapestry needle

▥ Two 1¾-inch/35mm decorative buttons (buttons from www.zecca.net)

GAUGE

14 sts and 20 rows to 4"/10cm over St st with size 10½ (6.5mm) needles before felting.

Take time to check gauge.

BOTTOM

With A, cast on 70 sts. Work in St st for 8"/20.5cm. Bind off.

SIDE PANELS

(make 2)

With A, cast on 32 sts. Working in St st, *work 4 rows with A, 4 rows with B; rep from * once more, work 4 rows with A. Then cont with B only until piece measures 15"/38cm from beg. K 5 rows. Bind off.

FRONT AND BACK PANELS

(make 1 each)

With A, cast on 70 sts. Complete as for side panels.

Shoulder strap

With B, cast on 12 sts. Working in St st, *work 8 rows B, 8 rows A; rep from * 13 times more. Work 8 rows B. Bind off.

Handles

(make 2)

With dpn and B, cast on 4 sts. Work 5 rows in St st. Cut yarn and set piece aside With another dpn and B, cast on 4 sts. Work 5 rows in St st. Hold the 2 pieces with p sides tog and with third dpn, k1 st from 1 dpn tog with 1 st from 2nd dpn—4 sts with 2 pieces joined.

***Next row (RS)** K4, do not turn. Slide sts to beg of needle to work next row from RS. Bring yarn around from back to k sts from this position. Rep from * for I-cord for 8"/20.5cm.

Next row Inc 1 st in each st across—8 sts. Working on first sts only, work 5 rows in St st. Bind off. Work rem 4 sts in st st for 5 rows. Bind off.

Work bobbles in A on back and side panels (the side panel bobble is worked in the center of the B section, the front and back bobbles are worked foll diagram). To make bobble, with tapestry needle and A, embroider a ¾"/2cm bobble by making a cross then embroider all around to form a circle. Sew bottom of bag to sides, and front and back pieces to sides. Center straps on bag sides, overlapping bag with the first 2 strips and sew in place. Sew on handles at center of bag using the two 4-st flaps to secure handles on RS and WS of back and front pieces.

Felting

Put finished bag in washing machine with small amount of dishwashing liquid. Wash in hot water with warm water rinse. Put through several cycles, if necessary, to the desired felted fabric. Put bag through a final rinse in cold water, with no agitation. Remove bag and straighten it by laying flat. Dry bag over a cardboard cut to fit inside bag, if desired, for a better definition of the dimensions. Run a line of straight sts all around the seams for more secure edges. Sew on buttons as in photo.

Diagram

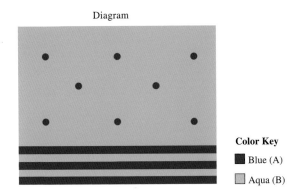

Color Key

■ Blue (A)

☐ Aqua (B)

BABY BONNET AND BOOTIES

Tiny treasures

Horseshoe lace and faggoting insets enhance this traditional bonnet and bootie set. Designed by Evelyn Clark, they make a perfect Christening day accessory or gift.

SIZES
Instructions are written for size 3-6 months.

KNITTED MEASUREMENTS
■ Bonnet measures 11½"/29cm around face edge
■ Booties fit a 4"/10cm length foot

MATERIALS
■ 2 1¾oz/50g balls (each approx 190yd/175m) of Dale of Norway Baby *Ull* (wool) (1)
■ One pair size 2 (2.75mm) needles *or size to obtain gauge*
■ 1 set (4) size 2 (2.75mm) dpn

GAUGE
32 sts and 44 rows to 4"/10cm over St st using size 2 (2.75mm) needles.
Take time to check gauge.

HORSESHOE LACE PATTERN
(multiple of 8 sts plus 3)
Row 1 (RS) Sl 1 knitwise wyib, k1, *yo, k2, SK2P, k2, yo, k1; rep from *, end k1.
Row 2 and all even rows Sl 1 purlwise wyif, purl to end.
Row 3 Sl 1, k2, *yo, k1, SK2P, k1, yo, k3; rep from * to end.
Row 5 Sl 1, k2, *k1, yo, SK2P, yo, k4; rep from * to end
Row 6 Rep row 2. Rep these 6 rows for horseshoe lace pat.

BONNET
Beg at face edge with size 2 (2.75mm) needles, cast on 91 sts.
Row 1 (RS) Sl 1, knitwise wyib, knit to end.
Row 2 Rep row 1. Then beg with row 1 of pat, work in horseshoe lace pat until rows 1-6 have been repeated 3 times. Then cont in faggoting st by rep rows 5 and 6 of pat only a total of 14 times more. Rep rows 1 and 2 once.
Crown shaping
Row 1 (RS) Sl 1, k42, ssk, p1, k2tog, k20, ssk, turn.
Row 2 Sl 1, p43, p2tog, turn.
Row 3 Sl 1, k19, ssk, p1, k2tog, k19, ssk, turn.
Row 4 Sl 1, p41, p2tog, turn.
Row 5 Sl 1, k18, ssk, p1, k2tog, k18, ssk, turn.
Row 6 Sl 1, p39, p2tog, turn.
Row 7 Sl 1, k17, ssk, p1, k2tog, k17, ssk, turn.
Row 8 Sl 1, p37, p2tog, turn.
Row 9 Sl 1, k16, ssk, p1, k2tog, k16, ssk, turn.
Row 10 Sl 1, p35, p2tog, turn.
Row 11 Sl 1, k15, ssk, p1, k2tog, k15, ssk, turn.
Row 12 Sl 1, p33, p2tog, turn.

Row 13 Sl 1, k14, ssk, p1, k2tog, k14, ssk, turn.
Row 14 Sl 1, p31, p2tog, turn.
Row 15 Sl 1, k13, ssk, p1, k2tog, k13, ssk, turn.
Row 16 Sl 1, p29, p2tog, turn.
Row 17 Sl 1, k12, ssk, p1, k2tog, k12, ssk, turn.
Row 18 Sl 1, p27, p2tog, turn.
Row 19 Sl 1, k11, ssk, p1, k2tog, k11, ssk, turn.
Row 20 Sl 1, p25, p2tog, turn.
Row 21 Sl 1, k10, ssk, p1, k2tog, k10, ssk, turn.
Row 22 Sl 1, p23, p2tog, turn.
Row 23 Sl 1, k9, ssk, p1, k2tog, k9, ssk, turn.
Row 24 Sl 1, p21, p2tog, turn.
Row 25 Sl 1, k8, ssk, p1, k2tog, k8, ssk, turn.
Row 26 Sl 1, p19, p2tog, turn.
Row 27 Sl 1, k7, ssk, p1, k2tog, k7, ssk, turn.
Row 28 Sl 1, p17, p2tog, turn.
Row 29 Sl 1, k6, ssk, p1, k2tog, k6, ssk, turn.
Row 30 Sl 1, p15, p2tog, turn.
Row 31 Sl 1, k5, ssk, p1, k2tog, k5, ssk, turn.
Row 32 Sl 1, p13, p2tog, turn.
Row 33 Sl 1, k4, ssk, p1, k2tog, k4, ssk, turn.
Row 34 Sl 1, p11, p2tog, turn.
Row 35 Sl 1, k3, ssk, p1, k2tog, k3, ssk, turn.
Row 36 Sl 1, p9, p2tog, turn.

Row 37 Sl 1, k2, ssk, p1, k2tog, k2, ssk, turn.
Row 38 Sl 1, p7, p2tog, turn.
Row 39 Sl 1, k1, ssk, p1, k2tog, k1, ssk, turn.
Row 40 Sl 1, p5, p2tog.
Row 41 Sl 1, ssk, p1, k2tog, ssk, turn.
Row 42 Sl 1, p3, p2tog, p1.
Bind off rem 7 sts.

I-cord ties and trim
With dpn, cast on 3 sts.
*Row 1 (RS) K3. Slide sts to beg of needle to work next row from this position. Bring yarn around from back of work and rep from * until I-cord measures 9"/23cm. Then attach I-cord for back trim as foll:
Next row (RS) K2, then working into back edge of bonnet (with the 7 bound-off sts at center of piece), sl last st on dpn and k1 st through the slipped st at edge of bonnet, pass slipped st over this st. Rep this row in every st along edge to the center 7 sts, then work into every other bound-off st, then cont along opposite edge as before. When trim is attached to back of bonnet, cont on the 3 sts in I-cord as before for 9"/23cm for other tie. Bind off.

FINISHING
Block bonnet flat.

BOOTIES
Beg at cuff edge with dpn, cast on 40 sts. Divide sts with 16 sts on needle 1, 8 sts on needle 2 and 16 sts on needle 3. Join, being careful not to twist sts. Pm for beg

of rnds. P 1 rnd, k 1 rnd.

Beg horseshoe lace pat

Rnd 1 *K1, yo, k2, SK2P, k2, yo; rep from * around.

Row 2 and all even rnds Knit.

Rnd 3 *K2, yo, k1, SK2P, k1, yo, k1; rep from * around.

Rnd 5 *K3, yo, SK2P, yo, k2; rep from * around.

Rnd 6 Knit.

Rep these 6 rnds twice more. K 2 rnds.

Next (eyelet) rnd *K2tog, yo; rep from * around. K 1 rnd, repositioning sts so that last 2 sts of needle 1 are at beg of needle 2 and first 2 sts of needle 3 are at end of needle 3. There are 14 sts on needle 1, 12 sts on needle 2 and 14 sts on needle 3.

Instep shaping

Row 1 K26, turn.

Row 2 Sl 1, p11, turn.

Row 3 Sl 1, k11, turn.

Rep rows 2 and 3 nine times more. Do not turn at end of last row.

Join sides

Cont across row with needle 3, pick up and k10 sts along left side of instep, k rem 14 sts.

Next rnd With needle 1, k14 then pick up and k10 sts along right side of instep, k to end of rnd—60 sts. There are 24 sts on needle 1, 12 sts on needle 2 and 24 sts on needle 3. Rejoin and k 12 rnds.

Sole

Rnd 1 and all odd rnds Purl.

Rnd 2 Knit.

Rnd 4 Ssk, k22, k2tog, k8, ssk, k22, k2tog—56 sts.

Rnd 6 Ssk, k21, k2tog, k6, ssk, k21, k2tog—52 sts.

Rnd 8 Ssk, k20, k2tog, k4, ssk, k20, k2tog—48 sts.

Rnd 10 Ssk, k19, k2tog, k2, ssk, k19, k2tog—44 sts.

Rnd 12 Ssk, k18, k2tog, ssk, k18, k2tog—40 sts.

Rnd 13 Purl.

Transfer the first st on needle 2 to the end of needle 1 and last st on needle to to beg of needle 3. Turn bootie inside out between these 2 needles and with 3rd needle, work 3-needle bind-off (see page 77) over the 20 sts from each needle.

Block booties lightly.

Twisted cords

(make 2)

Cut 1 strand of yarn 80"/203cm long, twist cord to measure approx 14"/36cm and pull through eyelet rnd. Knot ends of cords.

ARAN PULLOVER

Go fish!

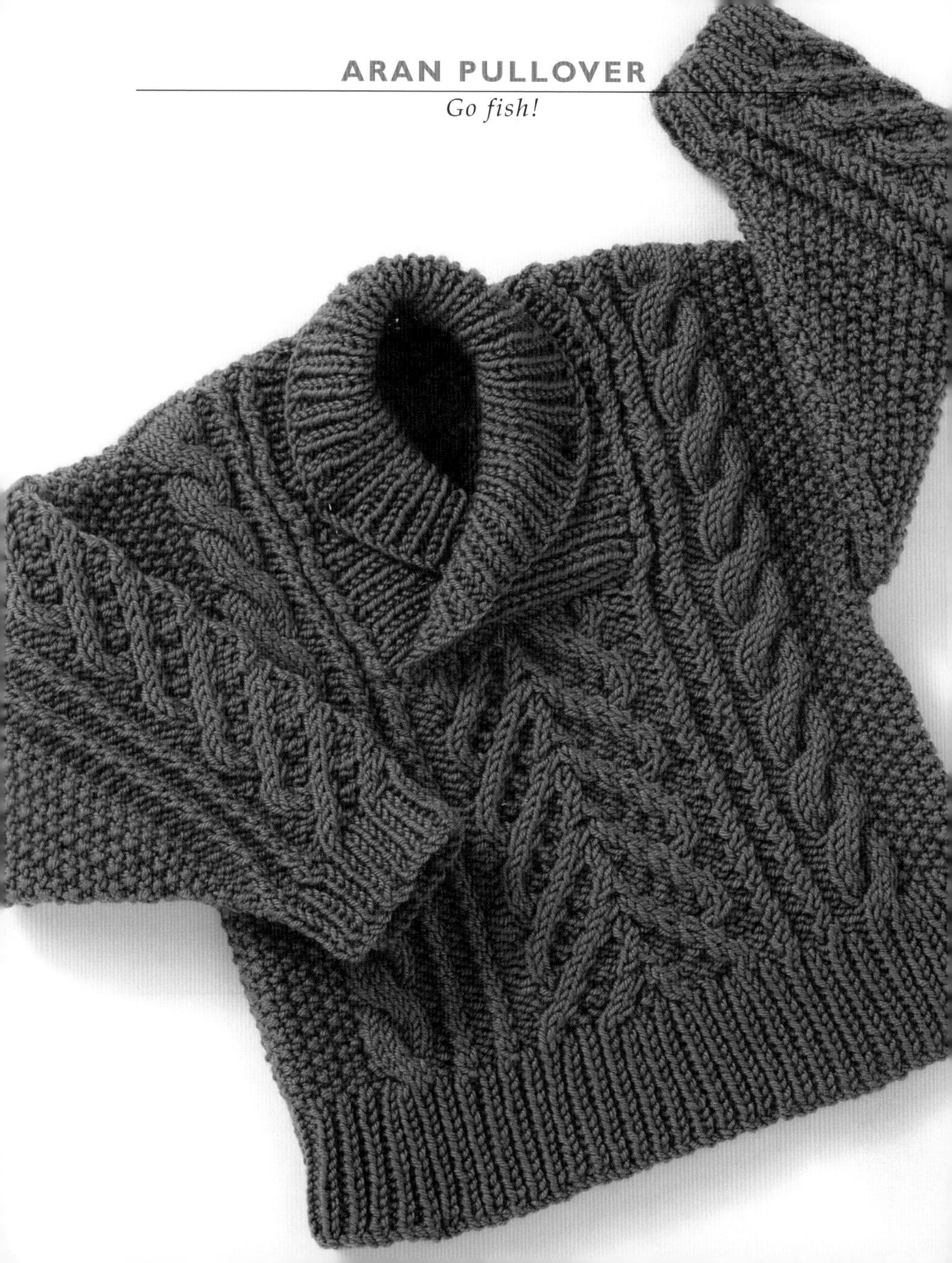

Scaled down cable patterns separated by simple seed stitch and rope cables are the key design elements of this classic Aran Isle baby sweater. A foldover shawl collar completes the look. Designed by Sara Harper.

SIZES
Instructions are written for size 6 months. Changes for sizes 12, 18 and 24 months are in parentheses.

KNITTED MEASUREMENTS
▨ Chest 18 (20, 24, 26)"/46 (51, 61, 66) cm
▨ Length 10 (11, 12, 14)"/25.5 (28, 30.5, 35.5) cm
▨ Upper arm 10 (10½, 11, 11)"/26 (27, 28, 28) cm

MATERIALS
▨ 4 (4, 5, 5) 1¾oz/50g balls (each approx 171yd/158m) of Le Fibre Nobili/Plymouth Yarn *Merino* (wool) in #4029 blue (④)
▨ One pair size 4 (3.5mm) needles *or size to obtain gauge*
▨ Size 4 (3.5mm) circular needle 16"/40cm long
▨ Stitch holders
▨ Stitch markers
▨ Cable needle

GAUGE
28 sts and 38 rows to 4"/10cm over seed st using size 4 (3.5mm) needles.
Take time to check gauge.

STITCH GLOSSARY
Right twist (RT) Sl 1 st to cn and hold to *back*, k1, k1 from cn.
Right purl twist (RPT) Sl 1 st to cn and hold to *back*, k1, p1 from cn.
Left twist (LT) Sl 1 st to cn and hold to *front*, k1, k1 from cn.
Left purl twist (LPT) Sl 1 st to cn and hold to *front*, p1, k1 from cn.
4-st RC Sl 2 sts to cn and hold to *back*, k2, k2 from cn.
4-st LC Sl 2 sts to cn and hold to *front*, k2, k2 from cn.
6-st RC Sl 3 sts to cn and hold to *back*, k3, k3 from cn.
6-st LC Sl 3 sts to cn and hold to *back*, k3, k3 from cn.

SEED STITCH
Row 1 *K1, p1; rep from * to end.
Row 2 K the purl and p the knit sts.
Rep row 2 for seed st.

BACK
Cast on 74 (80, 96, 104) sts. **Row 1 (RS)** *K1, p1; rep from * to end. Rep row 1 for k1, p1 rib for 1½ (1½, 2, 2)"/4 (4, 5, 5)cm.

Beg chart pat

Row I (RS) Work 9 (12, 10, 14) sts in seed st, sts 7-16 of chart 0 (0, 1, 1) time, sts 1-56 once, sts 41-50 0 (0, 1, 1) time, work 9 (12, 10, 14) sts in seed st. Cont to foll chart in this way, with sts outside of chart in seed st, rep rows 1-8 of chart until piece measures 9½ (10½, 11½, 13½)"/24 (26.5, 29, 34)cm from beg.

Neck shaping

Next row (RS) Work 23 (26, 34, 34), join a 2nd ball of yarn and bind off center 28 (28, 28, 36) sts, work to end. Working both sides at once, work until piece measures 10 (11, 12, 14)"/25.5 (28, 30.5, 35.5)cm from beg. Place sts on holders.

FRONT

Work as for back until piece measures 6 (6½, 7, 8)"/15 (16.5, 18, 20.5)cm from beg.

Neck opening

Next row (RS) Work 23 (26, 34, 34) sts, join a 2nd ball of yarn and bind off center 28 (28, 28, 36) sts, work to end. Working both sides at once, work even until same length as back to shoulders. Place sts on holders.

SLEEVES

Cast on 40 sts. Work in k1, p1 rib for 1 (1, 1½, 1½)"/2.5 (2.5, 4, 4) cm, inc 4 sts evenly across last WS row—44 sts.

Beg chart pat

Row I (RS) Beg with st 7, work through st 50 of chart. Cont to foll chart in this way, inc 1 st each side (working inc'd sts in seed st) every 2nd row 8 (9, 11, 0) times, every 4th row 9 (10, 10, 21) times—78 (82, 86, 86) sts. Work even until piece measures 7 (7½, 8, 11½)"/18 (19, 20.5, 29)cm from beg. Bind off loosely in pat.

FINISHING

Block lightly to measurements. Place matching shoulder sts on parallel needles and from WS, work 3-needle bind-off. (see page 77).

Collar

With circular needle, beg at right front corner of neck edge, pick up and k 88 (96, 104, 124) sts evenly around neck edge, ending at inside left front corner. Working back and forth in rows, work in k1, p1 rib for 3 (3, 3, 4)"/7.5 (7.5, 7.5, 10)cm or until collar fits across front neck bound-off opening. Bind off in rib. Sew end of collar to neck opening overlapping right side over left for girls, or left side over right for boys. Place markers at 5 (5¼, 5½, 5½)"/13 (13.5, 14, 14)cm down from shoulder for sleeves. Sew sleeves to armholes between markers. Sew side and sleeve seams.

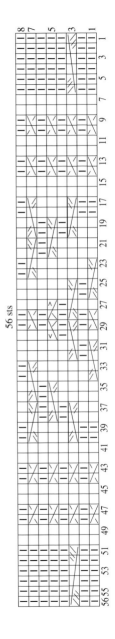

56 sts

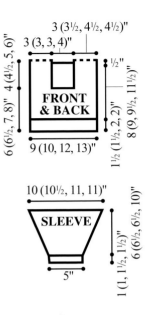

3 (3½, 4½, 4½)"
3 (3, 3, 4)"
½"

FRONT & BACK

6 (6½, 7, 8)" 4 (4½, 5, 6)"

9 (10, 12, 13)"

8 (9, 9½, 11½)"

1½ (1½, 2, 2)"

10 (10½, 11, 11)"

SLEEVE

6 (6½, 6½, 10)"

5"

1 (1, 1½, 1½)"

Stitch Key

$\boxed{1}$	k on RS, p on WS
$\square$	p on RS, k on WS
RT symbol	RT
LT symbol	LT
RPT symbol	RPT
LPT symbol	LPT
4-ST RC symbol	4-ST RC
4-ST LC symbol	4-ST LC
6-ST RC symbol	6-ST RC
6-ST LC symbol	6-ST LC

Fortunate cookie

Honoring the traditions of China, this baby set is knit primarily in red, symbolizing happiness and good fortune. The Chinese symbols "Xi" (joy) and "Shou" (longevity) are knit into the hem, reflecting a double blessing. Designed by Jennifer Lindsay.

SIZES

Instructions are written for One Size, size 12 months.

KNITTED MEASUREMENTS

Jacket
- Chest 23"/58cm
- Length 11"/28cm
- Upper arm 10"/26cm

Pants
- Hip 22"/56cm
- Length 13½"/34cm

Cap
- 16½"/42cm head circumference

MATERIALS

- 4 2oz/70g skeins (each approx 122yd/113m) of La Lana Wools *Dos Mujeres* (mohair/wool) in red (A)
- 3 2oz/70g skeins (each approx 142yd/131m) of La Lana Wools *Phat Silk Fines* (wool/silk) in *black* (B)
- 1 skein in gold (C)
- 1 1oz/28g skein (each approx 2yd/60m) of La Lana Wools *Lincoln Thickspun* (wool) in *gold* (D)
- One each sizes 4 (3.5mm) circular needles, 24"/60cm and 32"/80cm long; size 5 (3.75mm) 32"/80cm long *or size to obtain gauge*
- One set each (5) sizes 3 and 4 (3.25 and 3.5mm) dpn
- Stitch markers

GAUGES

- 24 sts and 32 rows to 4"/10cm over St st using size 5 (3.75mm) needles
- 25 sts and 40 rows to 4"/10cm over quilted lattice pat using size 4 (3.5mm) needles
- 27 sts and 29 rows to 4"/10cm over fretted band pat using size 5 (3.75mm) needles.

Take time to check gauges.

STITCH GLOSSARY

Quilted lattice
(over a multiple of 6 sts plus 3)
Row 1 (WS) and all WS rows Purl.
Row 2 K2, *sl 5 sts wyif, k1; rep from *, end k1.
Row 4 K4, *insert needle under the loose strand and k the next stitch, bringing this st out under strand; k5; rep from *, end last rep k4.
Row 6 K1, sl 3 sts with wyif, *k1 sl 5 sts wyif; rep from *, end k1, sl 3 sts wyif, k1.
Row 8 K1, k the next st under the loose strand, k5; rep from *, end last rep k1.
Rep rows 1-8 for quilted lattice.

Fretted Band
(over a multiple of 6 sts plus 2 with colors B and C)

Rows 1 and 2 With B, knit.

Row 3 (RS) With C, k6, *sl 1, k5; rep from *, end sl 1, k1.

Row 4 and all WS rows K the same sts worked on the previous row with the same color, slipping all the slipped sts, but with the yarn held in front.

Row 5 With B, k1, sl 1, *k3, sl 1, k1, sl 1; rep from *, end last rep k2, instead of k1, sl 1.

Row 7 With C, k4, *sl 1, k1, sl 1, k3; rep from *, end last rep k1.

Row 9 With B, k3, *sl 1, k1, sl 1, k3; rep from *, end last rep k2.

Row 11 With C, k4, *sl 1, k5; rep from *, end sl 1, k3.

Row 12 Rep row 4.

JACKET– BODY

With longer size 4 (3.5mm) circular needle and A, cast on 183 sts. Do not join. Work back and forth in rows. Work in St st for 5 rows.

Picot turning row (WS) P2, *yo, p2tog; rep from *, end p1. K 1 row, p 1 row.

Change to size 5 (3.75mm) circular needle.

Beg chart pat

Row 1 (RS) K1, work 28-st rep a total of 6 times, work sts 1-13 once more, k1. Cont to foll chart in this way through row 22.

Next row (RS) K3, pm, k55, pm (marking side seam), k67 (for back), pm, k55, pm, k3. P 1 row.

Neck shaping

Row 25 (RS) With A, k3, sl marker, k2tog, *k1C, k3A; rep from* to last 6 sts, k1C, with A, ssk, sl marker, k3. Cont to foll chart through row 29, keeping first and last 3 sts and decs in A, cont to dec 1 st at each marker every row (with k2tog then ssk on RS rows and p2tog tbl then p2tog on WS rows). After chart is completed, there are 53 sts in each of left and right fronts and 67 sts in back.

Change to longer size 4 (3.5mm) needles and cont with A, work in St st (with neck decs on each row) for 2 rows. Cut yarn. Rejoin A to work next row from RS.

Beg quilted lattice pat

Next row (RS) K3, sl marker, k5, k2tog, rep from * of row 2 of quilted lattice pat, end sl 5 wyif, k5, ssk, sl marker, k3.

Next row Purl, working WS row neck decs as before. Cont in this way, dec 1 st at markers for neck every row as before until row 8 of quilted lattice pat is completed. Work row 1 of pat again.

DIVIDE FOR FRONTS AND BACK

Pat row 2 (RS) K3, sl marker, k2tog, work next 37 sts in pat, bind off 3 sts for armhole (removing marker), work next 62 sts in pat, bind off 3 sts for armhole (removing marker), work next 36 sts in pat, ssk, sl marker, k3. There are 42 sts on each front and 63 sts on back.

LEFT FRONT

Working on left front sts only and leaving rem sts on hold to be worked later, cont neck decs every row until 20 sts rem. Then cont to dec 1 st every other row 4 times more. Work even on 16 sts until armhole measures 5½"/14cm.

Shoulder shaping

Bind off 8 sts from armhole edge twice.

RIGHT FRONT

Work as for left front, reversing shaping.

BACK

Work even on the 63 back sts until same length as fronts to shoulder.

Shoulder shaping

Bind off 8 sts at beg of next 4 rows. Bind off rem 31 sts.

SLEEVES

With shorter size 4 (3.5mm) circular needle and B, cast on 38 sts. Work 12 rows of fretted band pat. K 2 rows with B, inc 1 st on last row—39 sts. Change to A and beg on a WS row, work in quilted lattice pat inc 1 st each side every 4th row once, every other row 5 times, every 4th row 4 times, every 6th row 3 times—65 sts. Work 7 more rows (end with row 1 of pat). Sleeve measures approx 7"/18cm from beg. Bind off.

FINISHING

Block pieces to measurements. Turn up hem and sew in place. Sew shoulder seams. Sew sleeves into armholes. Sew sleeve seams.

Front band

With longer size 4 (3.5mm) circular nee-dle and B, pick up and k 79 sts to shoulder seam, 30 sts across back neck, 79 sts to lower edge—188 sts. K 1 row. Beg with row 3, work in fretted band pat through row 12. K 2 rows with B. Bind off loose-ly. Block band flat.

Interior ties

To secure wrap of jacket on the inside, cut 3 strands each of A, B and C 18"/45cm long. Secure to inside right underarm seam and braid ends; knot end. Work an opposite tie at inside left front band, beg at neck shaping.

I-cord (make 2)

With smaller dpn and B, cast on 3 sts.

***Row 1** Knit. Do not turn. Slide sts to opposite end of needle to work next row from RS. Bring yarn around from back and rep from * until I-cord measures 8½"/22cm. Change to C and work for 1"/2.5cm more. Bind off. Knot ends and attach one I-cord at right front beg of neck shaping and one I-cord at left underarm seam to correspond.

PANTS

Legs (make 2)

With size 3 (3.25mm) dpn and B, cast on 24 sts. Work in garter st for 12 rows. Cut yarn. Make a 2nd piece in same way. Then join 2 pieces on shorter size 5 (3.75mm) circular needle as foll: p23, p last st of first piece tog with first st of 2nd piece, p23—47 sts. Then cont to work back and forth, work in St st inc 1 st each side every 6th row once, every 4th row 16 times—81 sts. P 1 row.

Crotch shaping

Bind off 4 sts at beg of next 2 rows, 2 sts at beg of next 2 rows. Pm to mark this row. Work even until piece measures 5¾"/14.5cm from marker. Change to size 3 (3.25mm) dpn and work 5 more rows. K 1 row on WS for turning ridge. Work 5 more rows in St st. Bind off.

FINISHING

Block to measurements. Sew center and crotch seams. Sew side leg seams leaving open at garter border each side for side slits. Fold waistband to WS over elastic. Pull up elastic to fit and sew in place and secure.

CAP

With size 5 (3.5mm) circular needle and B, cast on 86 sts. Working back and forth in rows, work in fretted band pat for 12 rows. K2 rows B, inc 1 st on last row—87 sts. Change to A. Beg on row 1 (WS), work in quilted lattice pat rows 1-8 twice, rows 1-5 once. With C, k 1 row. With D, k 1 row, p 1 row. With A, purl, dec 7 sts evenly spaced—80 sts. Divide sts evenly onto 4 size 4 (3.5mm) dpn. Join to work in rnds.

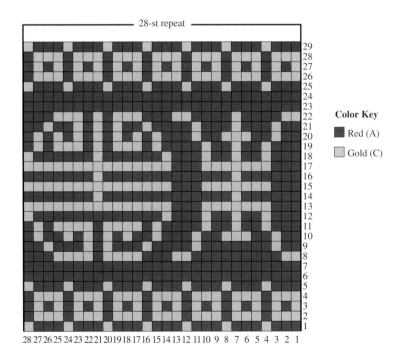

28-st repeat

Color Key

■ Red (A)

▨ Gold (C)

28 27 26 25 24 23 22 21 20 19 18 17 16 15 14 13 12 11 10 9 8 7 6 5 4 3 2 1

Rnd 1 *K2tog, k8; rep from * around—72 sts.

Rnd 2 Knit.

Rnd 3 *K2, k7; rep from * around—64 sts.

Rnd 4 Knit.

Cont to dec 8 sts in this way every other rnd 5 times more—24 sts. Then, dec 8 sts in this way every rnd twice more—8 sts. Cut yarn and pull through sts tightly to fasten off.

I-cord

With smaller dpn and B, cast on 3 sts. Work on I-cord for 3"/7.5cm. SK2P. Fasten off. Fasten I-cord to top of hat and knot.

Jacket

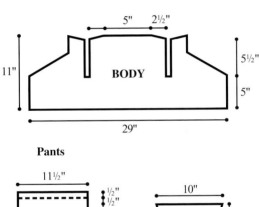

Pants

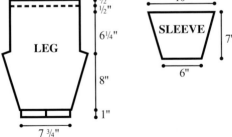

Frilly edges, floral insets and button back yoke work together in a dress that's perfect for your little girl. Designed by Sasha Kagan.

SIZES
Instructions are written for one size, size 6 months.

KNITTED MEASUREMENTS
- Chest 19"/48cm
- Length 13"/33cm
- Upper arm 7¾"/19.5cm

MATERIALS
- 3 1¾oz/50g balls (each approx 191yd/175m) of Rowan Yarns *4-Ply Soft* (wool) in #378 mauve (A)
- 1 ball each in #370 lt blue (B), #376 white (C), #387 grey (D), #379 green (E) and #375 periwinkle (F)
- Two pairs size 2 (2.75mm) needles *or size to obtain gauge*
- Four ⅜"/10mm buttons
- Bobbins (optional)

GAUGE
28 sts and 40 rows to 4"/10cm over St st using size 2 (2.75mm) needles.
Take time to check gauge.

Note
If desired wind yarn onto bobbins to make working floral pat foll chart easier.
Take time to check gauge.

RUFFLE PATTERN
Cast on sts as required.
Row 1 (RS) K1, *k2, sl first st over 2nd st on RH needle; rep from * to end.
Row 2 P1, *p2tog; rep from * to end.
Rows 3-6 Work in St st.

BACK
Under ruffle
With F, cast on 525 sts. Work rows 1-6 of ruffle pat—132 sts. Cut yarn and sl sts to a spare needle.

Top ruffle
With A, cast on 525 sts. Work rows 1-4 of ruffle pat—132 sts.

Next row With both needles tog with A over F ruffles in left hand, using A, join ruffle tog by knitting 1 st tog from each needle. With A, purl 1 row.

Beg chart pat
Row 1 (RS) Work 22-st rep of chart row 1 a total of 6 times. Cont to foll chart through row 20. Then cont with A only for 7½"/19cm above the chart band.

Separate for back opening
Next row (RS) K65, leave rem sts on hold to be worked later. Cont on these 65 sts for 1½"/4cm, end with a RS row.

Dec row (WS) P2, [p2tog] 31 times, p1 – 34 sts. Leave these sts on a spare needle.

Yoke ruffle
With F, cast on 133 sts. Work in ruffle for 4 rows as before—34 sts. Using F, join ruffle to sts from back. P 1 row.

Beg chart pat
Next row (RS) Work 1 st in D, then work 22 sts of chart pat, end with st 11. Cont to

foll chart in this way through row 4 of chart.

Armhole shaping

Next row (RS) Bind off 2 sts, work to end. P 1 row.

Next row (RS) K2tog, k to end. P 1 row. Rep last 2 rows twice more—29 sts. Cont to foll chart through row 20 then work rows 1-9 once more.

Neck shaping

Next row (WS) Bind off 10 sts, work to end. Cont to shape neck binding off 4 sts once more—15 sts. Work even for 3 rows. Bind off. Rejoin yarn to center back and bind off center 2 sts, work to end. Work left half as for right half, reversing shaping.

FRONT

Work as for back to the yoke ruffle.

Dec row (WS) P2, [p2tog] 64 times, p2—68 sts.

Yoke ruffle

With F, cast on 273 sts. Work 4 rows and join to yoke sts as before—68 sts. P 1 row.

Beg chart pat

Next row (RS) Work 1 st in D, work row 1 of chart 22-st rep 3 times, work 1 st in D. Cont to foll chart in this way until there are same number of rows as in back yoke.

Armhole shaping

Bind off 2 sts at beg of next 2 rows, dec 1 st each side every other row 3 times—58 sts. Cont to foll chart until 27 rows of chart have been worked.

Neck shaping

Next row (RS) K22, join a 2nd ball of yarn and bind off next 14 sts, work to end. Working both sides at once, dec 1 st from each neck edge *every* row 7 times—15 sts rem each side. When same length as back, bind off rem sts each side for shoulders.

SLEEVES

With F, cast on 109 sts. Work ruffle pat rows 1-4—28 sts.

Next (inc) row (RS) [Inc 1 st] 27 times, k1—55 sts. Change to A and p 1 row. Then cont in St st for 3½"/9cm from the ruffle edge.

Cap shaping

Bind off 2 sts at beg of next 2 rows. Dec 1 st each side every other row 4 times—43 sts. Work even for 2 rows. Bind off.

FINISHING

Block pieces to measurements, being sure not to flatten ruffles. Sew shoulder seams.

Back trim

With F, pick up and k 38 sts along right back opening on back. K 4 rows. Bind off. Place markers for 3 buttons on band, the first one at ruffle, the other 2 at 1¼"/3cm intervals. Work other side in same way with buttonholes worked in row 2 by yo, k2tog opposite marker.

Neckband

With F, pick up and k 4 sts from band, 12 sts to shoulder, 32 sts across front neck, 12

sts to band, 4 sts from band—64 sts. K 1
row.

Next row K3, yo, k2tog, k to end. K 2
rows more. Bind off. Sew sleeves into
armholes. Sew side and sleeve seams. Sew
on buttons.

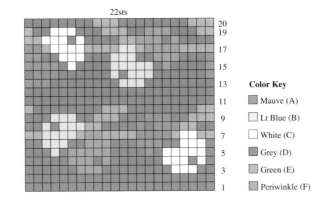

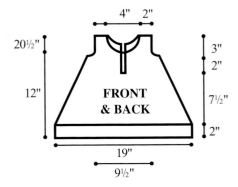

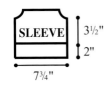

This whimsical homage to your favorite feline is the cat's meow. Designed by Wendy Bergman, it boasts bobble accents and dimensional ears.

SIZES

Instructions are written for size 6 months. Changes for sizes 12 and 24 months are in parentheses.

KNITTED MEASUREMENTS

▦ Head circumference 15 (17, 18½)"/38 (43, 47)cm
▦ Depth (with edge rolled) 5½ (5¾, 6)"/14 (14.5, 15)cm

MATERIALS

▦ 1 1¾oz/50g ball (each approx 87yd/81m) of Stahl Wolle/Skacel Collection *Big* (wool/acrylic) in #7931 black/white mix (A) ▦
▦ 1 ball in #7801 natural (B)
▦ Small amounts of pink (C) and lt grey (D) yarn for face
▦ One set (4) dpn size 6 (4mm) *or size to obtain gauge*
▦ Size 6 (4mm) circular needle 16"/40cm long (optional)
▦ Stitch markers

GAUGE

19 sts and 28 rows/rnds to 4"/10cm over St st using size 6 (4mm) needles.
Take time to check gauge.

Large bobble With color B, k into front, back, front and back of 1 st (for 4 sts in 1 st), turn. P4, turn. K4, turn. P4, turn. K2tog twice, turn. P2tog, then sl resulting st back to RH needle.

Small bobble With color B, k into front and back of 1 st (for 2 sts), turn. P2, turn. K2, turn. P2tog, then sl resulting st back to RH needle.

HAT

Note

If desired, entire hat may be worked using dpn. Or work with a circular needle until there are too few sts to work comfortably, then change to dpn.

With A and circular needle, cast on 72 (80, 88) sts. Join being careful not to twist sts. Pm to mark beg of rnd. Work in St st (k every rnd) for 2"/5cm.

Next rnd With A, k5 (6, 7), with B make large bobble, k with A until 6 (7, 8) sts from end of rnd, with B make large bobble, k with A to end of rnd.

Next rnd With A, k3 (4, 5), with B make small bobble, k3 with A, with B make small bobble, k with A until 8 (9, 10) sts from end of rnd, with B make small bobble, k3 with A, with B make small bobble, k with A to end of rnd.

Next rnd Work even with A.

Next rnd With A, k4 (5, 6), with B make small bobble, k1 with A, with B make small bobble, k with A until 7 (8, 9) sts from end of rnd, with B make small bobble, k1 with A, with B make small bobble, k with A to end of rnd.

Then cont to k every rnd with A only until piece measures 4¾ (5, 5¼)"/12 (12.5, 13.5)cm from beg, with edge unrolled. Change to B and k1 rnd.

Crown shaping

Note

When there are too few sts to fit circular needle, change to dpn.

Dec rnd *K6, SKP; rep from * to end— 63 (70, 77) sts. K 1 rnd.

Dec rnd *K5, SKP; rep from * to end— 54 (60, 66) sts. K 1 rnd.

Dec rnd *K4, SKP; rep from * to end— 45 (50, 55) sts. K 1 rnd.

Cont to work dec rnds every other rnd in this way 3 times more, having 1 st less before dec every dec rnd and 18 (20, 22) sts rem. Change to C.

Next rnd [SKP] 9 (10, 11) times—9 (10, 11) sts. K1 rnd with C.

Next rnd [SKP] 4 (5, 5) times, k1 (0, 1)—5 (5, 6) sts.

Draw yarn through rem sts on needles, pull up tightly and fasten off.

Note

Work back and forth in rows on 2 dpn. With A, cast on 8 sts. Work in St st (k 1 row, p 1 row) for 4½"/11.5cm. Change to B and cont for 1½"/4cm more. Bind off. Sew sides of rows tog to form tail, sewing the B section closed. Locate center back of hat (bobbles form the paws at center front) and sew end of tail to center back.

(make 2)

With B, cast on 7 sts. Working back and forth in rows with 2 dpn, work 4 rows in St st.

Next row (RS) K1, SKP, k1, k2tog, k1— 5 sts. P 1 row.

Next row SKP, k1, k2tog—3 sts. Draw yarn through rem sts and pull up lightly. Sew open ends of ears to hat, skipping one decreased wedge for top of head and sewing ears along 2 wedges at each side.

Using photo as a guide, embroider eyes, mouth and whiskers using D yarn and straight sts.

Brit pack

Classic argyle patterning pairs with grown-up V-neck styling to create a first vest that's perfect for your little boy or girl. Design is by Song Palmese.

SIZES
Instructions are written for size 6 months. Changes for sizes 12, 18 and 24 months are in parentheses.

KNITTED MEASUREMENTS
▨ Chest 22 (24, 26, 28½)"/56 (61, 66, 72.5)cm
▨ Length 11 (12, 12½ ,14)"/27.5 (30.5, 31.5, 35.5)cm

MATERIALS
▨ 2 (2, 3, 3) 1¾oz/50g balls (each approx 137yd/126m) of Anny Blatt *Merinos* (wool) in #31091 lt green (A) **3**
▨ 1 (2, 2, 2) balls in #33420 navy (B)
▨ One pair each sizes 3 and 5 (3.25 and 3.75mm) needles *or size to obtain gauge.*
▨ Size 3 (3.25mm) circular needle, 16"/40cm long

GAUGE
25 sts and 25 rows to 4"/10cm over St st and argyle pat foll chart using larger needles.
Take time to check gauge.

BACK
With smaller needles and A, cast on 69 (75, 81, 89) sts. Work in k1, p1 rib for 6 rows. Change to larger needles.
Beg chart pat
Row 1 (RS) Beg with st 1 (3, 5, 1) of row 1 of chart, work to rep line, work 10-st rep 6 (7, 8, 8) times, end with st 19 (17, 15, 19). Cont to work in St st and foll chart in this way, rep rows 1-12 until piece measures 6 (6½, 6½, 7½)"/15 (16.5, 16.5, 19)cm from beg.

ARMHOLE SHAPING
Bind off 4 (5, 6, 6) sts at beg of next 2 rows. Dec 1 st each side *every* row 7 (7, 8, 9) times—47 (51, 53, 59) sts. Work even until armhole measures 5 (5½, 6, 6½)"/12.5 (14, 15, 16.5)cm. Bind off.

FRONT
Work as for back until piece measures same as back to armhole. Shape armhole as on back. Work even on 47 (51, 53, 59) sts for 1 (1, 0, 1) row.
V-neck shaping
Next row (RS) Work 21 (23, 24, 27) sts, join a 2nd 2 balls of yarn and bind off center 5 sts, work to end. Working both sides at once, dec 1 st each side of neck *every* row 10 (8, 6, 6) times, every other row 5 (7, 9, 9) times—6 (8, 9, 12) sts rem each side. Work even until armhole measures same as back to shoulder. Bind off rem sts each side for shoulders.

Block pieces to measurements. Sew shoulder seams.

Armhole bands

With smaller needles and A, pick up and k 69 (76, 83, 89) sts around armhole edge. Work in k1, p1 rib for 5 rows. Bind off in rib. Sew side seams.

Neckband

With circular needle and A, pick up and k 78 (86, 90, 90) sts evenly around neck edge. Join and work in k1, p1 rib for 5 rnds. Bind off in rib.

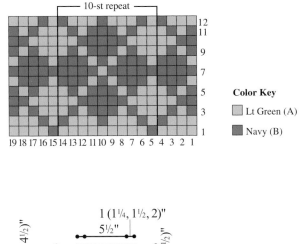

10-st repeat

12
11
9
7
5
3
1

19 18 17 16 15 14 13 12 11 10 9 8 7 6 5 4 3 2 1

Color Key

◻ Lt Green (A)

◼ Navy (B)

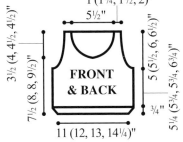

1 (1¼, 1½, 2)"

5½"

3½ (4, 4½, 4½)"

7½ (8, 8, 9½)"

5 (5½, 6, 6½)"

5¼ (5¾, 5¾, 6¾)"

¾"

FRONT & BACK

11 (12, 13, 14¼)"

Handknit bears with removable pajamas and slippers are of heirloom quality. Designed by Debbie Bliss, they're cuddly soft when knit in a cashmere blend yarn.

SIZES
Bear is 10½"/26cm tall.

MATERIALS
Bear
- 2 1¾oz/50g balls (each approx 84yd/78m) of Debbie Bliss/KFI *Merino Aran* (wool) in #103 tan (3)
- Small amount of dk brown yarn or embroidery floss
- One pair size 2 (2.75mm) needles *or size to obtain gauge*
- Polyester fiberfill for stuffing

PAJAMAS (BOYS)
- 1 1¾oz/50g ball (each approx 135yd/125m) of Debbie Bliss/KFI *Cashmerino Baby* (wool/microfiber/cashmere) each in #101 cream (A), #202 lt blue (B) and #203 dk blue (C) (3)
- One pair size 3 (3.25mm) needles *or size to obtain gauge*
- 3 small buttons
- Elastic thread for waist

PAJAMAS (GIRLS)
- 1 ball of *Cashmerino Baby* each in #101 cream (A), #602 dk pink (C) and small amounts in #600 lt pink (B) (3)
- One pair size 3 (3.25mm) needles *or size to obtain gauge*
- 3 small buttons
- Elastic thread for waist

GAUGES
Bear
- 32 sts and 48 rows to 4"/10cm over St st using Merino Dk and size 2 (2.75mm) needles

Pajamas
- 25 sts and 34 rows to 4"/10cm over St st using Cashmerino Baby and size 3 (3.25mm) needles.

Take time to check gauges.

BEAR
Legs
(make 2)
With size 2 (2.75mm) needles, cast on 38 sts. Beg with a K row, work 8 rows in St st.
Next row (RS) K19, turn. Work on this set of sts only. Dec 1 st at beg of next row and every other row twice more, then at end of next row—15 sts. Work 2 rows even.
Cut yarn and rejoin at inside edge to second set of sts, k to end. Dec 1 st at end of next row and every other row twice more, then at beg of next row—15 sts.
Work 2 rows even. P 1 row across all sts—30 sts. Work 14 rows even.
Next row (RS) K15, turn and work on this set of sts only.
Dec 1 st at each end of every row 3 times—9 sts. Work 1 row even. Bind off.
Rejoin yarn to rem sts and complete to correspond to first side.

Soles

(make 2)

Cast on 4 sts.

K 1 row. Inc 1 st at each end of every row twice, every other row twice. Work 9 rows even. Dec 1 st at each end of the next row and every other row twice, every row once—4 sts. Work 1 row even. Bind off.

Arms

(make 2)

Cast on 7 sts. Beg with a k row, work 2 rows in St st. Inc 1 st at each end of the next row and every other row once more. Work 1 row even. Inc 1 st at beg of the next row—12 sts. Work 1 row even. Cut yarn. Rep between *'s once. Inc 1 st at end of next row—12 sts. Work 1 row even.

K 1 row across all sts—24 sts. Inc 1 st at each end every other row once, every 6th row twice—30 sts. Work 11 rows even.

Next row (RS) K15, turn. Work on this set of sts only. Dec 1 st at each end of the next 3 rows—9 sts. Work 1 row even. Bind off. Rejoin yarn to rem sts and complete as first side.

Body

(make 2)

Cast on 5 sts. K 1 row. Inc 1 st at each end of the next 2 rows and every other row 3 times more—15 sts. Work 1 row even. Cut yarn. Rep between *'s once. K 1 row across both sets of sts, inc 1 st at each end of this row—32 sts. Work 19 rows even. Dec 1 st at each end of next row, every 4th row twice, every other row twice—22 sts. Work 1 row even. Bind off.

Back head

Cast on 5 sts. K 1 row. Inc 1 st at each end of next 2 rows, then at beg of the next 4 rows. Work 2 rows even. Inc 1 st at beg of next 2 rows—15 sts. Work 1 row even. Cut yarn. Bind on 5 sts. K 1 row.

Inc 1 st at each end of next 2 rows, then at end of the next 4 rows. Work 2 rows even. Inc 1 st at end of next 2 rows. 15 sts. Work 1 row even. Work 1 row across all sts—30 sts. Work 10 rows even.

Next row (WS) P15, turn. Work on this set of sts only. Dec 1 st at each end of next row and every 4th row once, every other row once. Dec 1 st at beg of next row.

Mark beg of last row. Dec 1 st at each end of next row and then at beg of foll row—5 sts. Work 1 row even. Bind off. Rejoin yarn at inside edge to rem sts, p to end.

Dec 1 st at each end of next row and every 4th row once, every other row once.

Dec 1 st at end of next row. Mark end of last row. Dec 1 st at each end of next row and then at end of foll row—5 sts. Work 1 row even. Bind off.

Head gusset

Cast on 15 sts. Work 6 rows in St st. Dec 1 st at each end of next row and every 4th row 3 times, every other row once. Work 3 rows even. Dec 1 st at each end of next row. Work 3 sts tog and fasten off.

Right side of head

Cast on 8 sts. K 1 row. Inc 1 st at beg of next row. Inc 1 st at each end of next row and at beg of the next 4 rows, then at end of next row. Inc 1 st at each end of next row, then at beg of the next row and end of next row—20 sts. Work 8 rows even. Mark end of last row. Bind off 2 sts at beg of next row. Work 1 row even. Dec 1 st at beg of next row and end of the foll row. Dec 1 st at each end of next row, then at end of the foll row. Dec 1 st at each end of next row and at end of foll row. Dec 1 st at each end of next row—8 sts. Work 1 row even. Mark beg of last row. Bind off.

Left side of head

Work as given for right side of head, reversing shaping.

Ears

(make 4)

Cast on 9 sts. Work 4 rows in St st. Dec 1 st at each end of next row and every other row once, every row once—3 sts. Bind off.

FINISHING

Join instep, top and inner back leg seams leaving an opening. Sew in soles. Stuff and close opening. Join arm seams, leaving an opening. Stuff and close opening. Join center seam on each body piece, join body pieces together, leaving bound-off edge open. Stuff and gather open edge, pull up and secure. Join sides of head from cast-on edge to first marker. Sew in head gusset, placing point at center front seam and cast-on edge in line with second markers on sides of head. Join center seams of back head, then sew to front head, matching markers and leaving cast on edge open. Stuff and gather open edge, pull up and secure. Sew head to body. Attach yarn approx ½"/1cm below top of one arm, thread through body at shoulder position, then attach other arm, pull yarn tightly and thread through body again in same place, then attach to first arm and fasten off. Attach legs in same way. Join paired ear pieces together and sew them in place. Embroider face features.

BOYS' PAJAMAS

JACKET–BACK

(Knitted sideways)

With A, cast on 26 sts. Beg with a k row, work in St st and stripe pat as foll: *1 row B, 1 row A, 1 row B, 1 row C, 1 row B, 1 row A, 1 row B, 3 rows A; rep from * (10 rows) for stripe pat for a total of 14 rows.

Neck shaping

Dec 1 st at beg of next row and at same edge every row twice—23 sts. Work 13 rows even.

Inc 1 st at neck edge on next 3 rows—26 sts. Work 14 rows even. Bind off with A.

LEFT FRONT

Work as for back to neck shaping.

Neck shaping

Bind off 4 sts at beg of next row. Dec 1 st at end of next row and at same edge every row twice more—20 sts. Work 6 rows even. Using A, k 3 rows. Bind off.

RIGHT FRONT

With A, cast on 19 sts. K 1 row.

Buttonhole row K2, [yo, k2tog, k4] twice, yo, k2tog, k3. K 1 row. Cont in St st and stripe pat. Work 6 rows even. Inc 1 st at the beg of next row and at same edge on next 2 rows. Work 1 row even. Cast on 4 sts at beg of next row—26 sts. Work 13 rows even. Bind off.

Join shoulder seams. Mark 24th st down from shoulder seam on back and front. With RS facing and A, pick up and k36 sts between markers. Beg with a p row work 2 rows in St st. Cont in St st and stripe pat as for back, dec 1 st at each end of 2nd row and every 4th row 3 times more—28 sts. With A, p 3 rows. Bind off purlwise.

Embroidery
With crochet hook, RS facing and beg at 4th st from edge, work vertical line of chain st in B, *skip 4 sts, then work another line of chain st; rep from * across width of work, omitting front borders.
Lower edge
With RS facing and A, pick up and k 50 sts along lower edge. K 2 rows. Bind off.
Collar
With RS facing and A, pick up and k 61 sts around neck edge. K 10 rows. Bind off. Join sleeve and side seams. Sew on buttons.

Legs
(make 2)
With A, cast on 8 sts. Work in St st for 2

rows. Cast on 18 sts at beg of next row—26 sts. Work 1 row even. Cont in St st and stripe pat as for back, work 48 rows. Bind off 18 sts at beg of next row. P 1 row. Bind off.
Embroidery
Embroider vertical lines to match Jacket.
Lower borders
With RS facing and A, pick up and k33 sts along lower edge. K 2 rows. Bind off.
Waist edging
With RS facing and A, pick up and k40 sts along waist edge.
Next row *K1, p1; rep from * to end. Rep the last row twice more. Bind off in rib.

Sew inner leg seam. Sew crotch seam. Thread elastic through waist to fit bear.

Jacket—Back, Fronts and Sleeves
Working with A throughout, work as given for boy's jacket.
Embroidery
Using split yarn, work flower centers in C and petals in B.
Lower edge
With RS facing and A, pick up and k50 sts along lower edge. K 1 row. With C, k 1 row, then bind off.
Collar
With RS facing and A, pick up and k61 sts

around neck edge. K 9 rows. With C, k 1 row, then bind off. Join sleeve and side seams. Sew on buttons.

TROUSERS

Legs

(make 2)

Working with A throughout, work as for boy's jacket.

Embroidery

Work to match jacket.

Lower borders

With RS facing and A, pick up and k33 sts along lower edge. K 1 row. With C, k 1 row, then bind off.

Waist edging

With RS facing and A, pick up and k40 sts along waist edge.

Next row *K1, p1; rep from * to end. Rep the last row twice more. Bind off in rib.

FINISHING

Sew inner leg seam. Sew crotch seam. Thread elastic through waist to fit bear.

SLIPPERS

(make 2)

With C, cast on 4 sts for sole.

K 1 row.

Cont in St st, inc 1 st at each end of next 2 rows, then every other row 3 times more—14 sts. Work 8 rows even. Dec 1 st at each end of next row then every other row 3 times more, then at each end of foll row—4 sts. Work 1 row even. Bind off. With C, cast on 42 sts. Beg with a k row, work 8 rows in St st.

Next row (RS) K24, k2 tog, turn.

Next row Sl 1, p6, p2 tog, turn.

Next row Sl 1, k6, p2 tog, turn. Rep the last 2 rows 3 times more, then work the first row again.

Next row Sl 1, k6, p2 tog, turn.

Next row K18, k2 tog, k to end. K 1 row. Bind off knitwise. Sew back seam. Sew in sole.

Make a small pompom and sew to front of slipper.

POMPOM TEMPLATE

Designed by Michelle Woodford, this pretty baby set features a snazzy pattern in her favorite color. Tassels on the hat lend a touch of whimsy.

SIZES

Instructions are written for size 3 months. Changes for sizes 6, 12 and 18 months are in parentheses.

KNITTED MEASUREMENTS

Pullover
- Chest 20 (22, 24, 26)"/51 (56, 61, 66)cm
- Length 11½ (12½, 13½, 14½)"/29.5 (32, 34, 36.5)cm
- Upper arm 9 (9, 10, 10)"/23 (23, 25, 25)cm

Pants
- Hip 19 (21½, 24, 26)"/48 (54.5, 61, 66)cm
- Length 14 (15, 16, 17)"/35.5 (38, 40.5, 43)cm

Hat (in 2 sizes)
- Head circumference 15 (17)"/38 (43)cm
- Depth 6 (6½)"/15 (16.5)cm

MATERIALS

- 6 (7, 7, 7) 1¾oz/50g hanks (each approx 85yd/78m) of Berroco, Inc *Cotton Twist* (cotton/rayon) in #8357 pink (A) ⟨4⟩
- 1 hank each in #8322 lime (C), #8330 blue (D) and #8327 lilac (E)
- 1 1¾oz/50g ball (each approx 77yd/71m) of Berroco, Inc *Chinchilla* (rayon) in #5101 white (B) ⟨4⟩
- One pair each sizes 7 and 8 (4.5 and 5mm) needles *or size to obtain gauge*
- Size 7 (4.5mm) dpn
- Size D/3 (3mm) crochet hook
- One ⅜-inch/10mm button
- ½yd/.5m of ½"/1cm wide elastic
- Stitch holders

GAUGE

19 sts and 23 rows to 4"/10cm over St st using larger needles.
Take time to check gauge.

GARTER STITCH STRIPE PATTERN

Row 1 (RS) With A, knit.
Rows 2 and 3 With B, knit.
Rows 4 and 5 With A, knit.
Rows 6 and 7 With C, knit.
Rows 8 and 9 With A, knit.
Rows 10 and 11 With D, knit.
Rows 12 and 13 With A, knit.
Rows 14 and 15 With E, knit.

PULLOVER

BACK

With larger needles and A, cast on 47 (53, 57, 61) sts. Work 15 rows of garter st stripe pat. Change to A and working in St st, work 3 (3, 5, 5) rows.

Note
K the first and last st of every row for selvage sts.

Beg chart pat

Row 1 (WS) Beg with st 1 (2, 2, 2), work 4-st rep a total of 11 (13, 14, 15) times, end with st 7 (6, 6, 6). Cont to foll chart in this way through row 26. Then cont in St st with A only until piece measures 7 (8, 8½, 9½)"/18 (20.5, 21.5, 24)cm from beg.

Armhole shaping

Bind off 2 (3, 2, 2) sts at beg of next 2 rows—43 (47, 53, 57) sts. Work even until armhole measures 2½ (2½, 3, 3)"/6.5 (6.5, 7.5, 7.5)cm.

Back neck opening

Next row (RS) Work 21 (23, 26, 28) sts, join a 2nd ball of yarn and bind off center st, k to end. Working both sides at once, work until armhole measures 4 (4, 4½, 4½)"/10 (10, 11.5, 11.5)cm.

Neck shaping

Bind off 8 (8, 9, 9) sts from each center neck edge—13 (15, 17, 19) sts rem each side. Always k the center neck st every row. Work even until armhole measures 4½ (4½, 5, 5)"/11.5 (11.5, 12.5, 12.5)cm. Bind off.

Work as for back (omitting neck opening) until armhole measures 3 (3, 3½, 3½)"/7.5 (7.5, 9, 9)cm.

Neck shaping

Next row (RS) Work 16 (18, 20, 22) sts, join a 2nd ball of yarn and bind off center 11 (11, 13, 13) sts, work to end. Working both sides at once, bind off 2 sts from each neck edge once, 1 st once—13 (15, 17, 19)

sts rem each side. Work even until same length as back. Bind off.

SLEEVES

With larger needles and A, cast on 29 (31, 35, 37) sts. Work 15 rows of garter st stripe pat.

Note

K the first and last st of every row for selvage sts. Change to A.

Next row (RS) With A, knit, inc 4 sts evenly spaced across—33 (35, 39, 41) sts. With A, work 2 rows in St st.

Beg chart pat

Next row (WS) Working row 16 of pat, beg with st 5 (7, 7, 5), work 4-st rep 8 (8, 9, 10) times, end with st 1. Cont to foll chart through row 26 only (then work with A to end of piece), AT SAME TIME, inc 1 st each side every 4th row 5 (4, 4, 3) times — 43 (43, 47, 47) sts. Work even until piece measures 6 (6½, 7, 7½)"/15 (16.5, 18, 19)cm from beg. Bind off.

FINISHING

Block pieces to measurements. Sew shoulder seams.

ONE-HALF COLLAR

Beg at center front neck, pick up and k 33 (33, 37, 37) sts evenly around to back neck opening. Work in k1, p1 rib for 1¼ (1¼, 1½, ½)"/3 (3, 4, 4)cm. Bind off in rib. Beg at center back neck opening, work other half collar in same way. Place markers at 4½ (4½, 5, 5)"/11.5 (11.5,

12.5, 12.5)cm down from shoulders. Sew sleeves to armholes between markers. Sew side and sleeve seam. With crochet hook, ch 5 for back neck buttonloop and attach under collar. Sew on button.

PANTS

Leg (make 2)

With larger needles and A, cast on 39 (43, 45, 47) sts. Work 15 rows of garter st stripe pat. Change to A.

Note K the first and last st of every row for selvage sts.

Next row (RS) Knit, inc 6 (6, 8, 8) sts evenly spaced across—45 (49, 53, 55) sts.

Next row Purl.

Next row Knit, inc 1 st each side of row —47 (51, 55, 57) sts.

Beg chart pat

Next row (WS) Working row 16 of pat, beg with st 7 (7, 7, 5), work 4-st rep 11 (12, 13, 14) times, end with st 1. Cont to foll chart in this way through row 26 only (then work with A to end of piece), AT SAME TIME, inc 1 st each side every 4th row 4 (5, 6, 7) times—55 (61, 67, 71) sts. Work even until piece measures 8 (9, 10, 10 ½)"/20.5 (23, 25.5, 26.5)cm from beg.

Crotch shaping

Bind off 3 sts at beg of next 2 rows.

Next row K1, k2tog, work to last 3 sts, SKP, k1. P 1 row. Rep last 2 rows once more—45 (51, 57, 61) sts. Work even until piece measures 14 (15, 16, 17)"/35.5 (38, 40.5, 43)cm from beg. Place sts on a holder. Work 2nd leg.

Waistband

Join all 90 (102, 114, 122) sts and with smaller needles, work in k1, p1 rib for 2"/5cm. Bind off in rib.

FINISHING

Block piece to measurements. Sew leg seams and crotch seam. Fold waistband over elastic cut to fit. Sew waistband in place and secure elastic.

HAT (sizes small and large)

With larger needles and A, cast on 35 (39) sts. Work 15 rows of garter st stripe pat. Change to A and working in St st, work 3 (5) rows.

Note K the first and last st of every row for selvage sts.

Beg chart pat

Next row (WS) Beg with st 7, work row 1 of chart pat working 4-st rep 8 (9) times, end with st 1. Cont to foll chart in this way through row 26, then rep rows 17-1 once more (this is the 2nd half of hat). With A, work 3 (5) rows even in St st. Then purling all the garter rows instead of knitting, work rows 15-2 of garter st stripe pat. P 2 rows with A. Bind off purlwise.

FINISHING

Block flat. Fold in half at top and sew side seams.

Tassels (make 2)

Using A, C, D and E, wind yarn 12 times around a 5"/2.5cm piece of cardboard. Slip a piece of A yarn through top and tie

up securely. Cut other end. Wind A
around tassel twice more as in photo. Trim
ends and attach to top corners of hat.

Color Key

■ Pink (A)

◎ White (B)

▢ Lime (C)

▢ Blue (D)

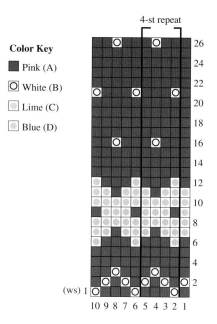

4-st repeat

(ws) 1

10 9 8 7 6 5 4 3 2 1

26 24 22 20 18 16 14 12 10 8 6 4 2

TASSELS
TASSELS
Cut a piece of cardboard to the desired
length of the tassel. Wrap yarn around the
cardboard. Knot a piece of yarn tightly around
one end, cut as shown, and remove the cardboard. Wrap and tie yarn around the tassel
about 1"/2.5cm down from the top to secure
the fringe.

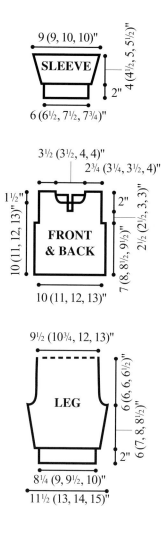

9 (9, 10, 10)"

SLEEVE

4 (4½, 5, 5½)"

2"

6 (6½, 7½, 7¾)"

3½ (3½, 4, 4)"

2¾ (3¼, 3½, 4)"

1½"

2"

**FRONT
& BACK**

10 (11, 12, 13)"

7 (8, 8½, 9½)"

2½ (2½, 3, 3)"

2½ (2½, 3, 3)"

10 (11, 12, 13)"

9½ (10¾, 12, 13)"

LEG

6 (6, 6, 6½)"

6 (7, 8, 8½)"

2"

8¼ (9, 9½, 10)"

11½ (13, 14, 15)"

GINGHAM BLANKET
Check mate

Double knitting stitch combines with a lightweight yarn to give this baby blanket its unique deep dimension and reversible style. Designed in a three-color gingham check pattern by Diane Zangl.

KNITTED MEASUREMENTS

▨ 32" wide x 30" long/81cm x 76cm

MATERIALS

▨ 2 6oz/70g skeins (each approx 290yd/265m) of Coats & Clark *Amoré* (acrylic/nylon) each in #3103 vanilla (A) and #3625 celery (B) (4)
▨ 1 skein in #3628 dk thyme (C)
▨ Size 7 (4.5mm) circular needles, 29"/74cm long *or size to obtain gauge*
▨ Bobbins (optional)

GAUGE

24 sts and 20 rows to 4"/10cm over double knit check pat using size 7 (4.5mm) needles. *Take time to check gauge.*

Notes

1 To work double knit check pat, carry both working colors in the same hand. Take both colors to the back when working a knit st and knit the color indicated. Bring both yarns to the front when working a purl st and purl the color indicated.

2 Carry color C up the side edge of the work, inside the border.

3 Slip first st of every row purlwise wyif.

4 Wind separate bobbins for each side border. To avoid holes while changing colors at borders, bring new color up over the old color.

5 Pattern stitch is reversible, with no RS or WS rows.

STITCH GLOSSARY

Double knit check pattern

Over a multiple of 6 sts plus 12 border sts.

Rows I and 3 With A, sl 1, k 5 (for border), [k1 with B, p1 with A] 3 times, *[k1 with A, p1 with B] 3 times, [k1 with B, p1 with A] 3 times; rep from *, end k6 with A (for border).

Rows 2 and 4 With A, sl 1, k5, [k1 with A, p1 with B] 3 times, *[k1 with B, p1 with A] 3 times, [k1 with A, p1 with B] 3 times; rep from *, end k6 with A.

Rows 5 and 7 With A, sl 1, k5, [k1 with C, p1 with B] 3 times, *[k1 with B, p1 with C] 3 times, [k1 with C, p1 with B] 3 times; rep from *, end k6 with A.

Rows 6 and 8 With A, sl 1, k5, [k1 with B, p1 with C] 3 times, *[k1 with C, p1 with B] 3 times, [k1 with B, p1 with C] 3 times; rep from *, end k6 with A. Rep rows 1-8 for double knit check pat.

With A, cast on 99 sts.
Row I Sl 1, knit to end.
Rep row 1 for 10 rows more.

Inc row With A, sl 1, k5, [k1, M1] 87 times, k6—186 sts. Cont in double knit check pat for 16 reps of pat. Work rows 1-4 of pat once more. Cut B and C.

Dec row With A, sl 1, k5, *sl 1 knitwise wyib, p1, psso; rep from * to last 6 sts, k6 —99 sts. Work even with A in garter st for 11 rows. Bind off loosely.

Allover seed stitch pattern teams with crunchy natural wool to make up this hooded outerwear jacket for Baby's fall wardrobe. The whimsical design is by Darlene Hayes.

SIZES

Instructions are written for size 6 months. Change for sizes 12, 18 and 24 months are in parentheses.

KNITTED MEASUREMENTS

⬛ Chest (closed) 23 (25, 27, 28¾)"/58.5 (63.5, 68.5, 73) cm

⬛ Length 11 (11½, 13, 14½)"/28 (29, 33, 37) cm

⬛ Upper arm 9½ (10½, 11½, 12¾)"/24 (26.5, 29, 32.5) cm

MATERIALS

⬛ 3 (3, 4, 4) 4oz/125g skeins (each approx 200yd/185m) of La Lana Wools *Silver Streak Millspun* (wool) in natural (**4**)

⬛ Sizes 5, 6 and 7 (3.75, 4 and 4.5mm) circular needles, 24"/60cm or straight needles, is desired

⬛ One set size 6 (4mm) dpn

⬛ Size G/6 (4.5mm) crochet hook

⬛ 2 sets of large hook and eye closures

⬛ Stitch holders

GAUGE

17 sts and 36 rows to 4"/10cm over seed st using size 7 (4.5mm) needles.
Take time to check gauge.

SEED STITCH PATTERN

Row 1 (RS) *K1, p1; rep from * to end.
Row 2 K the purl and p the knit sts.
Rep row 2 for seed st pat.

BODY

With size 7 (4.5mm) needles, cast on 96 (104, 112, 120) sts. Work in seed st pat until piece measures 5½ (5½, 6½, 7½)"/14 (14, 16.5, 19) cm from beg.

Divide for back and fronts

Next row (RS) Work first 24 (26, 28, 30) sts and sl to a holder for right front, semi cotton work next 48 (52, 56, 60) sts for back; sl rem 24 (26, 28, 30) sts to a st holder for left front. Work even on the 48 (52, 56, 60) sts for back for 5 (5½, 6, 6½)"/12.5 (14, 15, 16.5) cm. Place these sts on a holder.

RIGHT FRONT

Return to 24 (26, 28, 30) sts of right front and work even for 2½ (3, 3½, 4)"/6.5 (7.5, 9, 10)cm.

Neck shaping

Next row (RS) Bind off 3 (3, 4, 4) sts, work to end. Cont to shape neck dec 1 st at neck edge every other row 5 (6, 6, 6) times — 16 (17, 18, 20) sts. Work even until armhole measures 5 (5½, 6, 6½)"/12.5 (14, 15, 16.5)cm. Sl shoulder sts to a holder.

LEFT FRONT

Work as for right front, reversing neck shaping.

Hood

With size 7 (4.5mm) needles, cast on 43 (47, 51, 51) sts. Work in seed st for 6½ (7¼, 8, 9)"/16.5 (18.5, 20.5, 23)cm. Bind off 13 (14, 15, 15) sts at beg of next 2 rows—17 (19, 21, 21) sts. Work even on these sts for 3 (3¼, 3½, 3½)"/7.5 (8, 9, 9) cm or until side edges of this piece fit along the bound-off sts. Bind off in pat.

With size 7 (4.5mm) needles, cast on 24 (26, 28, 32) sts. Work in seed st, inc 1 st each side every 6th row 8 (9, 10, 11) times—40 (44, 48, 54) sts. Work even until piece measures 5½ (6¼, 7¼, 10)"/13 (16, 18.5, 25.5)cm from beg. Bind off loosely in pat.

Ties (make 4)

With 2 size 6 (4mm) dpn, cast on 4 sts.

*Row I K4, do not turn. Slide sts back to beg of needle and bring yarn around from front of needle to work from this position. Rep from * (for p-st I-cord) for 10"/26cm.

Next row Sl 1, k2tog, psso, then the last st over this st. Fasten off. Tie a knot at each end of tie.

Ears (make 2)

With size 5 (3.75mm) needles, cast on 11 sts. Work in seed st pat for 12 rows. Then cont in seed st dec 1 st each side on next row, then every 10th row once, every 6th row once, every 3rd row once —3 sts.

Next row Sl 2, k1, pass the 2 slipped sts over k st. Fasten off. With crochet hook, work an edge of the sc around entire inside portion of ear (so that ear folls to inside as in photo).

Block pieces to measurements. Using 3-needle bind-off, bind off back and front shoulder tog. Sew hood around neck edge. Fold ears in half. Insert ears, with ½"/1cm going to inside the top of hood where the top folds down to meet the bound-off edges. Seam the top of the hood, seaming through the doubled ears.

Corded edges

With size 6 (4mm) needles, pick up and k 26 (28, 30, 34) sts evenly along each sleeve cuff edge, [k1 row, p1 row] twice. Bind off. (This is a rolled reverse St st edge). With size 6 (4mm) needles, pick up and k 100 (108, 116, 124) sts evenly along lower edges of jacket. Work 4 rows corded edge as on sleeve cuff. With size 6 (4mm) circular, omitting lower bands, pick up and k132 (140, 156, 168) sts around center fronts and hood face edges. Work 4 rows corded edge as on sleeve cuff. Sew sleeves into armholes, stretching slightly to fit. Sew sleeve seams omitting rolled edges. Fasten 2 ties securely at neck edge and other 2 ties at 3"/7.5cm below. Sew on hook and eye under the ties.

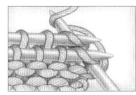

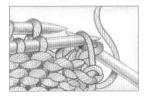

1 With RS placed together, hold pieces on two parallel needles. Insert a third needle knitwise into the first stitch of each needle, and wrap the yarn around the needle as if to knit.

2 Knit these two stitches together, and slip them off the needles. *Knit the next two stitches together in the same manner.

3 Slip the first stitch on the third needle over the second stitch and off the needle. Repeat from the * in Step 2 across the row until all stitches have been bound off.

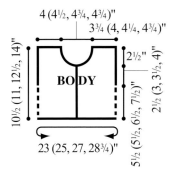

4 (4½, 4¾, 4¾)"

3¾ (4, 4¼, 4¾)"

10½ (11, 12½, 14)"

2½"

BODY

5½ (5½, 6½, 7½)"

2½ (3, 3½, 4)"

23 (25, 27, 28¾)"

9½ (10½, 11½, 12¾)"

SLEEVE

5½ (6¼, 7¼, 10)"

5½ (6, 6½, 7½)"

BABY BLUE OVERALLS
Locomotion

All aboard—a basic silhouette, buttoned closures and a playful motif are all it takes to create this easy-fit romper. Designed by Veronica Manno with a leg snap strip for easy changeability.

SIZES
Instructions are written for size 6 months. Changes for sizes 12, 18 and 24 months are in parentheses.

KNITTED MEASUREMENTS
- Chest 23 (24½, 26, 27½)"/58.5 (62, 66, 70)cm
- Length 18½ (20¼, 22, 23½)"/47 (51.5, 56, 59.5)cm

MATERIALS
- 3 (3, 4, 4) 1¾oz/50g balls (each approx 192yd/178m) of Sesia/LBUSA *Sesia Baby* (cotton) in #470 blue 🔷
- One pair size 6 (4mm) needles *or size to obtain gauge*
- Four ½-inch/13mm buttons
- 1yd/1m of ready-made snap fastener tape
- Matching blue thread
- Locomotive appliqué

GAUGE
20 sts and 30 rows to 4"/10cm over St st using size 6 (4mm) needles.
Take time to check gauge.

STITCH GLOSSARY
Dec 2 (RS rows)
Sl next 2 sts knitwise to RH needle, k next st, then pass 2 slipped sts, one at a time, over k st.

Dec 2 (WS rows)
Sl next 2 sts purlwise to RH needle, p next st, then pass 2 slipped sts, one at a time, over p st.

BACK
Left leg
Cast on 26 (28, 30, 32) sts.
Row 1 (RS) *K2, p2; rep from *, end k2 (0, 2, 0). **Row 2** K the knit and p the purl sts. Cont in k2, p2 rib for 2 rows more. Then cont in St st, inc 1 st at beg of every 4th row (RS rows for inside leg seam) 10 (10, 10, 12) times—36 (38, 40, 44) sts. Work even until piece measures 7 (8, 9, 9½)"/18 (20.5, 23, 24)cm from beg, end with a RS row. Set piece aside.
Right leg
Work as for left leg, reversing shaping with incs at end of rows.
Leg joining
Next row (WS) P35 (37, 39, 43) sts of left leg, p last st of leg tog with first st of right leg, p to end—71 (75, 79, 87) sts.
Next row (RS) K34 (36, 38, 42) sts, dec 2 (RS), k to end. Cont to dec 2 sts over the center 3 sts every row 4 (4, 4, 6) times more, every other row twice—57 (61, 65, 69) sts. Work even until piece measures 7 (7½, 8, 8½)"/18 (19, 20.5, 21.5)cm from the point of the leg joining.
Armhole shaping
Bind off 3 sts at beg of next 2 rows, 2 sts at beg of next 4 rows, dec 1 st each side every other row 4 times—35 (39, 43, 47) sts. Work even until armhole measures 3½ (3¾, 4, 4½)"/9 (9.5, 10, 11.5)cm.

Neck shaping

Next row (RS) Work 15 (16, 17, 18) sts, join a 2nd ball of yarn and bind off center 5 (7, 9, 11) sts, work to end. Working both sides at once, bind off 4 sts from each neck edge once, 3 sts once. When armhole measures 4½ (4¾, 5, 5½)"/11.5 (12, 12.5, 14)cm, bind off rem 8 (9, 10, 11) sts each side for shoulders.

FRONT

Work as for back until armhole measures 2½ (2¾, 3, 3½)"/6.5 (7, 7.5, 9)cm.

Neck shaping

Next row (RS) Work 15 (16, 17, 18) sts, join a 2nd ball of yarn and bind off center 5 (7, 9, 11) sts, work to end. Working both sides at once, bind off 3 sts from each neck edge once, 2 sts once and 1 st twice—8 (9, 10, 11) sts rem each side. Work even until piece measures same length as back.

Next row (RS) *[K2, p2] twice, k0 (1, 2, 2), p0 (0, 0, 1); rep from * on 2nd side.

Next (buttonhole) row *Rib 1 (2, 2, 2), yo, k2tog, rib 2 (2, 2, 3), yo, k2tog, rib to end; rep from * on 2nd side. Cont in k2, p2 rib for 2 rows more. Bind off in rib.

FINISHING

Block pieces to measurements. Sew side seams.

Armhole bands

Pick up and k 52 (54, 58, 62) sts evenly around armhole edge. Work in k2, p2 rib for 4 rows. Bind off in rib.

Back neckband

Pick up and k 32 (34, 36, 38) sts evenly along back neck edge. Work as for armhole bands.

Front neckband

Pick up and k 36 (38, 40, 42) sts and work as for back neckband.

Leg bands

Pick up and k 88 (100, 112, 118) sts evenly along back inside leg edge. Work in k2, p2 rib for 4 rows. Bind off in rib.

Work front leg bands in same way. Baste snap fastener tape to fit back leg opening. Baste tape in same way to front leg opening, being sure that snaps line up correctly. Sew tape in place with thread, cutting ends and seaming under for extra security.

Pocket

Cast on 18 sts. Work in St st for 14 rows. Then, work in k2, p2 rib for 3 rows. Bind off in rib. Sew pocket to center front. Sew appliqué on pocket.

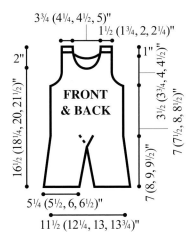

3¾ (4¼, 4½, 5)"

1½ (1¾, 2, 2¼)"

2"

1"

16½ (18¼, 20, 21½)"

FRONT & BACK

3½ (3¾, 4, 4½)"

7 (7½, 8, 8½)"

7 (8, 9, 9½)"

5¼ (5½, 6, 6½)"

11½ (12¼, 13, 13¾)"

This dynamic duo is perfect for a little boy and girl. The pink version offers girlie ruffles, while the blue features plain rib. Designed in a lush cashmere blend yarn by Veronica Manno.

Instructions are written for size 6 months. Changes for sizes 12 months, 18 months and 24 months are in parentheses.

KNITTED MEASUREMENTS
▥ Chest 19 (21, 23, 25)"/48 (53, 58.5, 63.5)cm
▥ Length 8½ (9 ½, 11, 13)"/21.5 (24, 28, 33)cm
▥ Upper arm 10 (10½, 11 11½)"/25 (27, 28, 29)cm

MATERIALS
▥ 2 (2, 3, 3) 1 ¾oz/50g balls (each approx 135yd/125m) of Debbie Bliss/KFI *Baby Cashmerino* (wool/microfiber/cashmere) each in #600 lt pink (A) (girls) or #202 lt blue (A) (boys) and #602 dk pink (B) (girls) or #203 dk blue (B) (boys) ⭐
▥ One pair size 3 (3.25mm) needles or *size to obtain gauge*
▥ Stitch holders

GAUGE
25 sts and 36 rows to 4"/10cm over St st using size 3 (3.25mm) needles.
Take time to check gauge.

STRIPE PATTERN
Working in St st, work: [8 rows B, 8 rows A] twice, [4 rows B, 4 rows A] twice, *2 rows B, 2 rows A; rep from * (4 rows) to end of piece.

GIRLS' VERSION
BACK
Beg ruffle With A, cast on 150 (165, 180, 195) sts.
Work in St st for 4 rows.
Dec row (RS) [K2tog, k3tog] 30 (33, 36, 39) times—60 (66, 72, 78) sts*. Then cont in St st and stripe pat until piece measures 8 (9, 10½, 12½)"/20.5 (23, 26.5, 32)cm from ruffle edge. Sl all sts to a holder.

FRONT
Work as for back until piece measures 6½ (7½, 8½, 10½)"/16.5 (19, 21.5, 26.5)cm from ruffle edge.
Neck shaping
Next row (RS) Work 22 (24, 26, 28) sts, place center 16 (18, 20, 22) sts on a holder, join a 2nd ball of yarn and work to end. Working both sides at once, place 1 st from each neck edge on a holder every other row 6 times—16 (18, 20, 22) sts rem each side. Work even until piece measures same as back. Sl sts from shoulders onto holders.

SLEEVES
With A, cast on 95 (100, 105, 110) sts. Work in St st for 4 rows.

Dec row (RS) [K2tog, k3tog] 19 (20, 21, 22) times—38 (40, 42, 44) sts*. Then cont in St st and stripe pat, inc 1 st each side every 4th (4th, 4th, 6th) row 12 (13, 13, 14) times—62 (66, 68, 72) sts. Work even until piece measures 6 (7, 8, 10)"/15.5 (17.5, 20.5, 25.5)cm from ruffle edge. Bind off.

FINISHING
Block pieces to measurements.

Buttonhole band
Working across sts from left front shoulder, with A, work 16 (18, 20, 22) sts. Work 2 rows in St st.

Buttonhole row Work 3 (3, 4, 4) sts, yo, k2tog, work 6 (8, 8, 10) sts, yo, k2tog, work 3 (3, 4, 4) sts. Work 2 more rows in St st. Bind off.

Button band
With A, work across corresponding 16 (18, 20, 22) sts from left back shoulder and work in St st for 5 rows. Using 3-needle bind-off (see page 77), bind off sts of right shoulder tog.

Neckband
With A, pick up and k12 sts from shaped front neck, work 16 (18, 20, 22) sts from front neck holder, pick up and k 12 sts from shaped front neck edge, work 28 (30, 32, 34) sts from back neck holder—68 (72, 76, 80) sts. Work in St st for 3 rows. Bind off.

Sew on buttons and button shoulder closed. Place markers at 5 (5¼, 5½, 5¾)"/12.5 (13.5, 14, 14.5)cm down from shoulders. Sew sleeves to armholes between markers. Sew side and sleeve seams.

BOYS' VERSION
Cast on with A, beg at *'s for the number of sts for back, front and sleeves, (that is, the number of sts after dec'ing for ruffles), work in k1, p1 rib on these sts for 4 rows then cont as for girls' version.

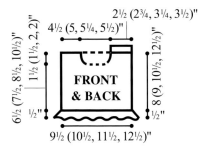

2½ (2¾, 3¼, 3½)"
4½ (5, 5¼, 5½)"
6½ (7¼, 8½, 10½)"
1½ (1½, 2, 2)"
FRONT & BACK
8 (9, 10½, 12½)"
½"
½"
9½ (10½, 11½, 12½)"

10 (10½, 11, 11½)"
SLEEVE
6 (7, 8, 10)"
½"
6 (6½, 6¾, 7)"

Knit this pullover with raglan sleeves for your child's next play date. Ingenious patch pocket house boasts a roof top flap to stash your tot's favorite belongings. Designed by Lila Chin.

SIZES
Instructions are written for size 6 months. Changes for sizes 12, 18 and 24 months are in parentheses.

KNITTED MEASUREMENTS
■ Chest 20 (22½, 24½, 27)"/51 (57, 62, 68.5)cm
■ Length (with edge rolled) 10¼ (11¼, 13½, 15)"/26 (28.5, 34, 38)cm
■ Upper arm 8½ (9¼, 10, 10¾)"/21.5 (23.5, 25.5, 27)cm

MATERIALS
■ 2 (2, 3, 3) 3½oz/100g balls (each approx 207yd/188m) of Lion Brand Yarn Co. *Cotton Ease* (cotton/acrylic) in #157 yellow (A) **4**
■ 1 ball each in #107 blue (B), #102 pink (B), #133 orange (C) and #148 turquoise (D)
■ One pair each sizes 6 and 7 (4 and 4.5mm) needles *or size to obtain gauge*
■ Size 6 (4mm) circular needle, 16"/40cm long
■ One ½-inch/13mm button
■ Size F/5 (3mm) crochet hook
■ Stitch markers

GAUGE
20 sts and 28 rows to 4"/10cm over St st using larger needles.
Take time to check gauge.

BACK
With smaller needles and A, cast on 50 (56, 62, 68) sts. Work in St st for 1"/2.5cm. Change to larger needles and cont in St st until piece measures 6 (6½, 8, 9)"/15 (16.5, 20.5, 23) cm from beg, with edge unrolled.

Raglan armhole shaping
Bind off 3 sts at beg of next 2 rows.
Dec row (RS) K1, SKP, work to last 3 sts, k2tog, k1. Rep dec row every other row 4 (5, 7, 8) times more, [every 4th row once, every other row once] 3 times, every other row 0 (1, 2, 3) times, AT SAME TIME, when armhole measures 1¾ (2, 2½, 3)"/4.5 (5, 6.5, 7.5)cm and there are 34 (38, 40, 44) sts work as foll:
Separate for neck opening
Next row (RS) Work to center 4 sts, k2, join a 2nd ball of yarn and k to end.
Next row (WS) P to last 2 sts of first side, k2; k2 on 2nd side, p to end. Cont in this way, with 2 sts in garter st each side of neck opening and cont with raglan decs as before until 11 (12, 12, 13) sts rem each side. Work even, if necessary, until armhole measures 4¼ (4¾, 5½, 6)"/11 (12, 14, 15)cm. Bind off 2 k sts from left border and sl rem 9 (10, 10, 11) sts to a hold-

85

er for left edge and 11 (12, 12, 13) sts for right edge to a holder.

Work as for back, omitting the neck opening, until there are 28 (30, 30, 32) sts left after raglan armhole shaping.

Neck shaping

Next row (RS) Cont raglan shaping, work to center 14 (16, 16, 18) sts and place these center sts on a holder for neck, join a 2nd ball of yarn and work to end. Cont raglan shaping and working both sides at once, dec 1 st from each neck edge (beg k2tog, k1 on the right side and k1, SKP on the left side) every other row 4 times. Fasten off last st on each side.

With smaller needles and A, cast on 26 (28, 30, 32) sts. Work in St st for 1"/2.5cm. Change to larger needles and cont in St st, inc 1 st each side [every 4th once, every 6th row once] 4 (4, 5, 5) times, then every 4th row 0 (1, 0, 1) time more—42 (46, 50, 54) sts. Work even until piece measures 7½ (8½, 9½, 11)"/19 (21.5, 24, 28)cm from beg, with edge unrolled.

Raglan cap shaping

Bind off 3 sts at beg of next 2 rows.

Dec row (RS) K1, SKP, work to last 3 sts, k2tog, k1. Rep dec row every other row 4 (5, 7, 8) times more, [every 4th row once, every other row once] twice, every other

row 3 (4, 4, 5) times—12 sts. Sl these sts to a holder.

Block pieces to measurements, being careful not to unroll lower edges. Set sleeves into armholes.

Neckband

With circular needle and MC, work across sts from holders and 5 sts from each shaped neck edge—68 (72, 72, 76) sts. Work back and forth in rows in St st for 1"/2.5cm. Bind off. Sew side and sleeve seams. With crochet hook, work a chain 8 buttonloop on left back neck edge. Sew on button opposite loop.

House pieces

With larger needles and B, cast on 17 sts. Work in St st for 2¾"/7cm. Then work in garter st for 4 rows. Bind off knitwise.

Door

With larger needles and B, cast on 10 sts. Work in garter st for 1"/2.5cm. Bind off.

Roof

Beg at top edge, with larger needles and C, cast on 7 sts. K1 row, then work in garter st, inc 1 st at beg of *every* row 12 times—19 sts. Cont in garter st until piece measures 2"/5cm from beg. Bind off.

Chimney

With larger needles and D, cast on 1 st. Work in garter st, inc 1 st at end of every other row 4 times—5 sts. Cont in garter st until piece measures 1"/2.5cm from beg.

Bind off. Center house at 1½ (2, 2½, 3)"/4 (5, 6.5, 7.5)cm from lower edge (with edge unrolled) and sew to sweater on 3 sides with top opening along garter edge for pocket. Sew door to center and embroider knob with D using a French knot. Sew on roof with opening over the house pocket. Sew on chimney.

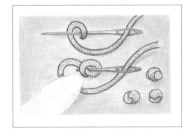

FRENCH KNOT

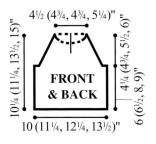

4½ (4¾, 4¾, 5¼)"

10¼ (11¼, 13½, 15)"

FRONT & BACK

4¼ (4¾, 8, 9)"

6 (6½, 8, 9)"

10 (11¼, 12¼, 13½)"

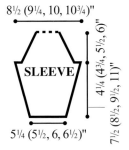

8½ (9¼, 10, 10¾)"

SLEEVE

4¼ (4¾, 5½, 6)"

7½ (8½, 9½, 11)"

5¼ (5½, 6, 6½)"

Springtime violets adorn this pretty baby set. With classy curved hemline on the cardigan and garter stripes trimming edges all around, it's designed by Gayle Bunn in a lightweight cotton yarn.

SIZES

Instructions are written for size 6 months. Changes for size 12 months are in parentheses.

KNITTED MEASUREMENTS

Cardigan
▥ Chest (closed) 20½ (22½)"/52 (57)cm
▥ Length 11 (11¾)"/28 (30)cm
▥ Upper arm 9 (10)"/23 (25.5)cm
Booties
▥ Foot measures 4½ (5)"/11.5 (12.5)cm

MATERIALS
▥ 3 1¾oz/50g balls (each approx 136yd/125m) of Patons® Grace (cotton) in #60322 purple (A) **2**
▥ 1 ball each in #60005 white (B), #60104 blue (C) and #60027 green (D)
▥ One pair size 5 (3.75mm) needles or *size to obtain gauge*
▥ Three ⅝-inch/15mm buttons

GAUGE
24 sts and 32 rows to 4"/10cm over St st using size 5 (3.75mm) needles.
Take time to check gauge.

GARTER STRIPE PATTERN
Rows 1-4 With A, knit.
Rows 5-8 With D, knit.
Rows 9-12 With A, knit.
Rows 13 and 14 With C, knit.
Rows 15 and 16 With B, knit.
Rows 17 and 18 With C, knit.
Rep these 18 rows for garter stripe pat.

CARDIGAN

BODY
With A, cast on 101 (113) sts.
Beg chart pat
Row 1 (RS) Work sts 1-8 of chart, work 12-st rep 7 (8) times, end with st 29 of chart. Cont to foll chart in this way inc 1 st each side *every* row 10 times—121 (133) sts. Then cont to foll chart rows 12-45. When row 45 is completed, rep rows 36-45 (for dot pattern) to end of piece, AT SAME TIME, when piece measures 5½ (5¾)"/14 (14.5) cm from beg, separate for armholes as foll:

RIGHT FRONT
Next row (RS) Work 26 (29) sts (for right front), leave rem sts on hold to be worked later. Working on right front sts only, work 1 row even.
Next (dec) row (RS) Work to last 2 sts, k2tog (armhole edge).
Rep dec row every other row once more—24 (27) sts. Work 1 row even.

Neck shaping

Next row (RS) Dec 1 st (neck edge), work to end of row. Cont to dec 1 st for neck every other row 6 (9) times more, every 4th row 3 (2) times—14 (15) sts. Work even until armhole measures 4¼ (4¾)"/11 (12)cm, end with a RS row.

Shoulder shaping

Bind off 7 sts from shoulder edge once, 7 (8) sts once.

BACK

Return to next set of sts on hold and rejoin yarn, bind off 6 sts (for armhole), work until there are 57 (63) sts on needle (for back), leave rem sts on hold. Work 1 row even. **Next row (RS)** Dec 1 st each side of row. Work 1 row even. Rep last 2 rows once more—53 (59) sts. Work even until armhole measures same as right front.

Shoulder shaping

Bind off 7 sts at beg of next 2 rows, 7 (8) sts at beg of next 2 rows. Bind off rem 25 (29) sts for back neck.

LEFT FRONT

Rejoin yarn to work rem sts, bind off 6 sts for armhole, work to end. Complete as for right front, reversing shaping.

SLEEVES

With A, cast on 8 sts for sleeve cuff. Work garter stripe pat on these sts until piece measures approx 6½"/16.5cm, end with row 12 of pat.

Beg sleeve

Turn piece to side and with RS of garter stripes facing, using A, pick up and k41 (43) sts along side edge of cuff. P1 row, k1 row, p1 row.

Beg chart pat

Row 16 (RS) Beg with row 16 of pat and with st 7 (6), work to rep line, then work 12-st rep 3 times, end with st 23 (24). Cont to foll chart in this way, AT SAME TIME, inc 1 st each side of next RS row, then every 4th row 6 (7) times more—55 (59) sts. Work even (in dot pat) until piece measures 5½ (6¼)"/14 (16) cm from beg (measured from end of sleeve cuff).

Cap shaping

Bind off 7 sts at beg of next 6 rows. Bind off rem 13 (17) sts.

FINISHING

Block pieces to measurements. Sew shoulder seams.

Edging

With A, cast on 8 sts. Work in garter stripe pat until piece fits from back right side seam edge around lower back and left front edge to right shoulder seam, sewing (or basting) band in place while knitting. Place markers for 3 buttons along the left front edge, the first one at beg of curve, the last one at beg of neck shaping and the 3rd one evenly spaced between. Cont to knit band to fit right front working buttonholes opposite markers as foll:

Buttonhole row (RS) K3, bind off 2 sts, k3 on next row, cast on 2 sts over bound-off sts. Cont to work band until it fits entirely around outer edge. Bind off and sew seam in place. Sew sleeves into armholes. Sew sleeve seams. Sew on buttons.

BOOTIES

Cuff

With A, cast on 8 sts. Work in garter stripe pat for 5¾"/14.5cm, end with pat row 4. With RS facing and A, pick up and k36 sts along side edge (into rows) of cuff. Beg with a purl row, work 5 rows in St st.

Instep shaping

Next row K24, turn.

Next row P12, turn. Work 2 (4) more rows on these 12 sts, inc 1 st at center of last row—13 sts.

Beg chart pat

Next row (RS) Working row 16 of chart, work pat foll sts 2-14 of chart. Cont to foll chart in this way through row 26.

Next row (WS) With A, purl dec 1 st at center of row—12 sts. Work 4 more rows even with A. Cut yarn.

Sides

With RS facing, rejoin A at side edge of instep and pick up and k12 (14) sts along side of instep, k12 from sts on hold at end of instep, pick up and k12 (14) sts along other side of instep, k rem 24 sts—60 (64) sts. Beg with a P row, work in St st for 7 rows.

Sole shaping

Next row (RS) Sl first 24 (26) sts to RH needle, join A to center 12 sts and work 1 row in garter stripe pat on these sts. Cont in garter stripe pat as foll:

Next row K11, k2tog, turn.

Next row K11, ssk, turn.

Rep these 2 rows until 12 sts rem.

Next row K2tog across while binding off sts. Sew center back seam.

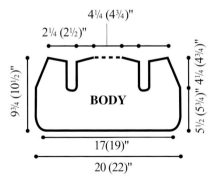

4¼ (4¾)"

2¼ (2½)"

9¾ (10½)"

5½ (5¾)" 4¼ (4¾)"

BODY

17(19)"

20 (22)"

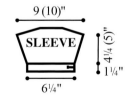

9 (10)"

SLEEVE

4¼ (5)"

4¼"

1¼"

6¼"

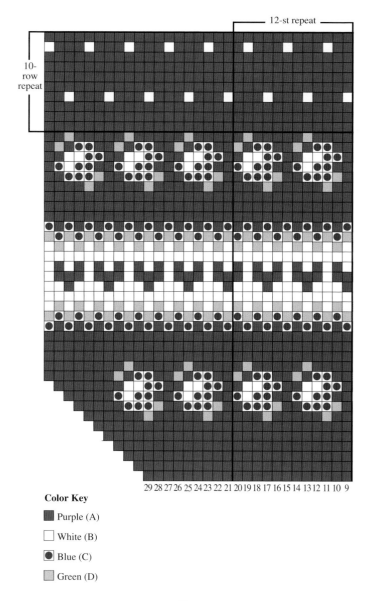

10-
row
repeat

29 28 27 26 25 24 23 22 21 20 19 18 17 16 15 14 13 12 11 10 9

Color Key

■ Purple (A)

☐ White (B)

◉ Blue (C)

▨ Green (D)

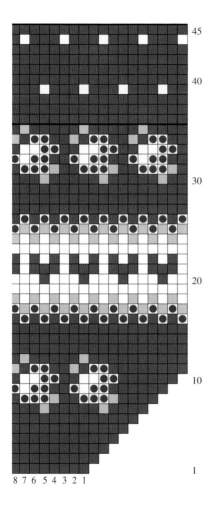

RESOURCES

US RESOURCES

*Write to the yarn
companies listed below for
purchasing and mail-order
information.*

ANNY BLATT
7796 Boardwalk
Brighton, MI 48116

BERROCO,INC.
P. O. Box 367
Uxbridge, MA 01569

BROWN SHEEP CO.
100662 County Road 16
Mitchell, NE 69357

CLASSIC ELITE YARNS
300A Jackson Street
Lowell, MA 01852

COATS AND CLARK, INC.
Attn: Consumer Service
PO Box 12229
Greenville, SC 29612-0229

DALE OF NORWAY
N16 W23390 Stoneridge Drive,
Suite A
Waukesha, WI 53188

DEBBIE BLISS
distributed by
KFI

GEDIFRA
distributed by
KFI

KFI
35 Debevoise Ave.
Roosevelt, NY 11575

LA LANA WOOLS
136 Paseo Norte
Taos, NM 87571

LBUSA
PO Box 217
Colorado Springs, CO 80903

LE FIBRE NOBILI
distributed by
Plymouth Yarn

LION BRAND YARN CO.
34 West 15th Street
New York, NY 10011

MANOS DEL URUGUAY
Distributed by Design Source
P.O. Box 770
Medford, MA 02155

PATONS® YARNS
PO Box 40
Listowel, ON N4W 3H3

PLYMOUTH YARN
PO Box 28
Bristol, PA 19007

ROWAN YARNS
4 Townsend West, Unit 8
Nashua, NH 03063

SESIA
distributed by
LBUSA

SKACEL COLLECTION, INC.
PO Box 88110
Seattle, WA 98138-2110

STAHL WOLLE
distributed by
Skacel Collection, Inc.

TAHKI YARNS
distributed by
Tahki•Stacy Charles, Inc.

TAHKI•STACY CHARLES, INC.
8000 Cooper Ave.
Brooklyn, NY 11222

CANADIAN RESOURCES

Write to US resources for mail-order availability of yarns not listed.

BERROCO, INC.
distributed by
S. R. Kertzer, Ltd.

CLASSIC ELITE YARNS
distributed by
S. R. Kertzer, Ltd.

DIAMOND YARN
9697 St. Laurent
Montreal, PQ H3L 2N1
and
155 Martin Ross, Unit #3
Toronto, ON M3J 2L9

PATONS ®
PO Box 40
Listowel, ON N4W 3H3

ROWAN
distributed by
Diamond Yarn

UK RESOURCES

Not all yarns used in this book are available in the UK. For yarns not available, make a comparable substitute or contact the US manufacturer for purchasing and mail-order information.

ROWAN YARNS
Green Lane Mill
Holmfirth
West Yorks HD7 1RW
Tel: 01484-681881

SILKSTONE
12 Market Place
Cockermouth
Cumbria, CA13 9NQ
Tel: 01900-821052

THOMAS RAMSDEN GROUP
Netherfield Road
Guiseley
West Yorks LS20 9PD
Tel: 01943-872264

VOGUE KNITTING BABY BLANKETS TWO

Editorial Director
TRISHA MALCOLM

Assistant Editor
MIRIAM GOLD

Art Director
CHI LING MOY

Book Division Manager
MICHELLE LO

Executive Editor
CARLA S. SCOTT

Production Manager
DAVID JOINNIDES

Instructions Editor
MARI LYNN PATRICK

Photography
QUENET STUDIOS

Knitting Editor
KAREN GREENWALD

Photo Stylist
LAURA MAFFEO

Yarn Editor
VERONICA MANNO

Graphic Designer
CAROLINE WONG

President, Sixth&Spring Books
ART JOINNIDES

LOOK FOR THESE OTHER TITLES IN THE *VOGUE KNITTING ON THE GO!* SERIES...